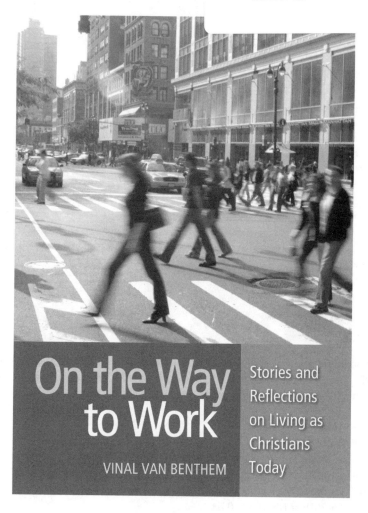

On the Way to Work

Stories and Reflections on Living as Christians Today

VINAL VAN BENTHEM

TWENTY-THIRD PUBLICATIONS

185 WILLOW STREET • PO BOX 180 • MYSTIC, CT 06355
TEL: 1-800-321-0411 • FAX: 1-800-572-0788
E-MAIL: ttpubs@aol.com • www.twentythirdpublications.com

Twenty-Third Publications
A Division of Bayard
185 Willow Street
P.O. Box 180
Mystic, CT 06355
(860) 536-2611 or (800) 321-0411
www.twentythirdpublications.com
ISBN:1-58595-291-5

Library of Congress Catalog Card Number: 2003113303
Printed in the U.S.A

Contents

Introduction

This book is one Christian laywoman's perspective on what it means to be a people of "the Way"; what it means to be a follower of Jesus Christ, who identifies himself as the Way; what it means to be a pilgrim people who travel the way; and what any of this could possibly have to do with working for a law firm in downtown Chicago.

Five years ago I gave my seminary students an assignment. Each week they were to write a short homily connecting the Sunday lectionary readings with the world of work. Since I believe that "the word of God is living and active" it seemed obvious that the Scriptures would naturally find application in the day-to-day lives of the people in the pews.

Some of my students, however, objected to the assignment. While they agreed generally that the Scriptures are as relevant to life today as they were when they were written, they were finding it difficult to make meaningful connections between the Sunday readings and life as it is lived in the workplace. I decided that, if I truly believed what I was asking them to preach, then I would have to take on my own assignment. That decision was the first step toward the book you now hold in your hand.

Two or three years previous to this time I had begun writing a parish bulletin column called "Working with the Scriptures." Each week I used an example taken from the workplace and attempted to connect it to the Scriptures. Now I decided to reverse the process. Instead of starting with the worker, I would start with the Word. Sometimes the example would flow out of the gospel, sometimes from one of the other readings.

Often what came out bore little if any resemblance to the homily Father preached on Sunday morning. At first I worried about that, concerned that I might be missing something. But then people began to stop by my office, and even call me on the phone, to thank me for helping them to connect their lives with the Scriptures in a way that they could finally understand. And people began to ask, "When are you going to put all of this together and write a book?"

Well, today is the day. To the people with whom I worked in downtown Chicago; to the spiritual directors and mentors who encouraged my passion for the spirituality of work; to my family, who made space in their lives so that my passion might have room to grow; to the Friars at St. Peter's Church in Chicago who made space in their home so that I might have a place and time to write; to all those people who read my words over the years and encouraged me to compile them into this volume; and to my students, many of whom are now ordained and preaching the Scriptures in ways that help their parishioners to understand God's Word as it relates to them in the world of their work, I say "Thank you."

This is my hope: that the stories you read and the people you meet in these pages will encourage you to begin making your own connections between what you hear proclaimed in church on Sunday and what you do on Monday. The Word of God must not be dismissed as simply the object of academic study or the subject of lunchtime discussion groups. In his Letter to the Hebrews Paul tells us that "the word of God is living and active...." Your assignment, then, is to listen so that you, too, may hear God's word, living and active, in your life and in your work. In the words of Francis of Assisi, "I have done what was mine to do—may Christ teach you what is yours...."

CHAPTER 1

Stories of Butchers, Bakers, and Other Working People

Hot rain,
early in the morning.

They walk,
her dress a farmer's garden
of dooryard flowers.

He, tall,
outdoor lines
trace life
across his face.

Each shelter for the other;
no need to speak.
Long years of words
let silence be enough.

His heavy feet
find dry place
on the earth.

She walks behind,
content to take
the path he claims
for both.

I saw the couple one morning while I was on my way to work. It was early July, and it was raining. I was hurrying to my office at St. Peter's in downtown Chicago. The sidewalk was crowded with commuters in beige trench coats making their way from the train station to offices and shops in the Loop. Everyone was rushing, it seemed, except these two people. They were walking directly in front of me and seemed curiously removed from the scene around them. While most of us were moving at a near run the man and the woman walked slowly. They did not speak to one another, but appeared to be in deep thought. I wondered what might have brought them here.

Had they come to see a lawyer? This part of town houses many of the city's law offices and accounting firms. Maybe they were seeking financial advice. Were they, like so many in these days of corporate farming, in danger of losing their farm? Or had they, perhaps, lost a child in a farming accident? Were they looking for help so that they might protect their remaining children financially? What burdens were these people carrying that would bring them into the city on such a hot and rainy morning?

And then other questions came into my mind. How would they be received by the professional from whom they were seeking advice? How would this couple—so obviously not accustomed to the life and pace of the city—be received by the receptionist who would greet them? Would she look up from her computer long enough to see the pain in their eyes? Would the accountant speak in words that would be understandable to these people who were grounded in a world where words were seldom spoken? Would the lawyer find time in her busy schedule to really listen to their story?

"The reign of God may be likened to a man who sowed good seed in his field" (Mt 13:24). Jesus often spoke in parables, and the parables often spoke of people who worked. As I walked behind the man with his weathered face and the woman in her cotton dress I thought about other working people—and other fields…

The Butcher

"It's different in the workplace. It's harder to sort out how gospel values work here."

His name is Fred. He's a butcher, a department manager in a small independent grocery store. In the years since Fred's hiring the owner of the store has developed a steadily increasing respect for his creativity and ambition. He is, both personally and professionally, an asset, and his boss is quick to acknowledge how much his presence has contributed to the growth of the business. By all accounts Fred is a young man on the way up. But there is one problem.

Another man has been with the owner since the store went independent some years ago. Until recently it was understood that this man would be made managing partner when the time came for the owner to retire from that role. While it's true that this man is not as productive as Fred is, he has put in long years of faithful service. Now it looks like a choice will have to be made between the two.

The long-term employee has stuck it out over the long haul. While he hasn't contributed much to the business, he has been loyal. Should the owner's response to him now be to deprive him of the promotion he has been looking forward to? How should the owner act toward the "good and faithful servant" (Mt 25:14–29)?

On the other hand, what about the young man hired "later in the day"? He has worked hard, and his hard work shows in increased profits and customer base. "'Lord, your pound has made ten more pounds'" (Lk 19:16). What reward might he expect for his efforts?

So we come back to where we began. The store owner is trying to be a good Christian. But it's different in the workplace. It's harder to sort out. How do we write the Scriptures of our days in the places where we work?

The Baker

He was a baker, an immigrant from northern Europe. He opened a bakery in a large midwestern city and became quite successful; but he always had time to share stories of the old country with his customers, and he treated his employees like extended family. Then he died.

The man's son took over the business but, instead of focusing on quality and fair business practices, his only goal was to make more money. He cut corners. He fired longtime employees. He substituted inferior ingredients for the rich butter and fine flour his father had insisted on using, and he no longer had time to visit with his customers. Employees found rats and bugs in the flour bins and the Health Department was called. The bakery's reputation, built on the old baker's hard work and care for customer and employee alike, was ruined by the son's greed. The bakery closed.

In his book, *spirituality@work*, Gregory F. Pierce describes what he calls the "ten disciplines of a spirituality of work." He defines one of them as "deciding what is 'enough'—and sticking to it," and responds to the question "What is enough?" with the old joke, "just a little bit more than I've got." The baker's son, and the rich man in Luke's parable (12:13–21), might have added "and I don't care what I have to do to get it."

In the culture of Jesus' time it was unthinkable that one should attempt to build up riches. People understood that resources were finite. If the needs of all were to be met no one could seek to have more than another, for if one person had more that meant that someone else had to have less. In the gospel story, however, the questioner is not satisfied with what he has. He wants what his brother has as well. Like the rich man in the story—and the baker's son—even though he has much, it still isn't enough.

How do we know when enough is enough? It's a good question, and one we might spend some time thinking about.

The Businessman

A gentleman I know recently moved to a large city on the East Coast to work in the home office of a firm with which he had been affiliated for several years. As is so often the case these days, the move wasn't his idea but, rather, a management decision. Still, he had worked with many of the people in the home office before and he anticipated an easy transition.

He was wrong. During what was for him a difficult time of adjustment he found himself virtually ignored by co-workers and people he thought might be friends in the new work environment. No one made any attempt to welcome him. There were no invitations to go to a ballgame or take in a movie. He had become just one more nameless face in a nameless workplace.

Have you ever found yourself in a situation like this? Perhaps, like my friend, you were the new person coming into the established culture. Or perhaps you were a member of the established culture into which a new person was introduced. Do you know the people with whom you work? Doctors? Lawyers? Indian chiefs? Do you know if that young executive and his wife have had their baby yet? Do you know if the secretary in the next carrel has recovered from her surgery? Do you know if her daughter got married? Or if his son has returned from his stint with the army?

There is in each one of us a deep need to be known, but all too often it goes unrecognized. Even Jesus in his humanity experienced this need to be known. He needed to be reassured that his disciples, those people with whom he lived and worked most closely, really knew him, and so he asked them "who do you say that I am?" (Lk 9:20).

Who are the people in your workplace? Do you know their names? Have you listened to their stories? "Who do you say that I am?"

The Haberdasher

There was a sign in the window of one LaSalle Street haberdashery that said, "shoes shined daily by Ron Anderson." Now, I don't know Ron Anderson, but I'd be willing to bet that he gives one heck of a shoeshine!

And the reason I'm so sure of that fact is that he's willing to be identified with his work. Think about it. "Contract by Mary Smith." "Audit by Jim James." "Food served by Lou French."

For many of us there seems to be a split between our work and the code of ethics with which we say we identify. And that split deepens when what we're talking about involves our faith. For some reason we often feel that the two must remain separate, that the way we live on Sunday has nothing whatsoever to do with the way we live the rest of the week. And while all of this might seem perfectly rational in the business world, it also seems to border on the schizophrenic! Unfortunately, it's a schizophrenia with which many of us are afflicted.

Since the advent of "piece work," it has become increasingly difficult for us to feel a sense of pride and accomplishment in what we do. Often this isn't so much because our work has no worth as it is that we do only a small part of a much larger project. The engineer is as necessary as the architect who is as necessary as the steelworker—and so on and so on. But while the building may say "Designed by..." no one of them can put his name on the finished project and claim it totally as his own.

Our life, however, is a different matter. We are, indeed, the sum of many parts. The hope is that our faith will be the thread from which the whole is woven. Our primary job is to fulfill the command to "Be perfect, therefore, as your heavenly Father is perfect" (Mt 5:48). Jesus isn't suggesting that we are to be perfect in the sense of having no flaw or sin. Rather, perfection in this case means wholeness, being "all of a piece," having integrity—in other words, the wholeness that is necessary for holiness. This is our job, twenty-four hours a day, seven days a week. This is the task we are given not just on Sunday but every day of our lives. When we know that we have done this job well, when we are sure that the product of our labor is the very best we have to offer, then we will not hesitate to have our name attached to it.

With what would you be willing to be identified? What would the sign in your window say?

The Tool and Die Maker

He was just a tool and die maker in a small machine shop on the northwest side of the city. Two men, partners, owned the operation. He was their foreman. Married. One daughter, all grown up now and married herself. She was just a child when they had hired him years earlier. Not social friends, exactly. But over the years they had become part of one another's lives. And now he had cancer.

They could lay him off. It would be the prudent thing to do. As it became more and more obvious that radiation and chemotherapy were robbing them of his work hours, it would only make good sense for them to begin to seek a replacement for him. And medical costs couldn't go anywhere but up. Their insurance rates would surely reflect this.

He died a few months later. They were both at the wake, and at the funeral. They held his wife and comforted his daughter. And they grieved the loss of a friend (Mt 5:4).

He was just a tool and die maker in a small machine shop on the northwest side of the city. Or maybe it was a carpenter shop…

The Doctor

He wasn't at all what they had expected (Mt 11:7–10). In the first place, "he" was a "she". When Dr. Creighton retired everyone had assumed that the doctor who was coming to take his place would be male. Dr. Creighton had explained that his practice would be taken over by a Dr. Terry Clement, but they had assumed that "Terry" stood for Terrence. What's more, some folks in town had heard that not only was the new doctor a woman, she was a *young* woman. Dr. Creighton had cared for three generations of people in the town. How could a young woman fresh out of medical school even begin to fill his shoes?

The people asked questions like, "Is she competent?" or "Can a young, unmarried woman handle the practice all alone?" A small group of disgruntled citizens even started a campaign to get rid of her. Responses to the arrival of the new young doctor included everything from Letters to the Editor to heated conversations in the back booth at the Corner Café. It seemed the whole town was talking.

That is, until the day that Mary Taylor lost her baby, and Dr. Terry Clement cried. She had done everything in her power to save the baby, but it hadn't been enough. And so she did the only thing she knew to do—she sat with Mary and her husband, and cried. The people didn't know what to make of it. Certainly Dr. Creighton had lost patients. Death was part of life. But Dr. Creighton had never cried. Dr. Creighton was compassionate but his medical training said that doctors simply did not cry.

Dr. Terry wasn't what the people had expected, and not all of them were happy about her arrival. Some even tried to use the loss of the Taylor baby to justify their attacks. But Mary and her husband knew better. Sitting together in silence that cold winter night they had known the presence of God in the gift of Dr. Terry Clement's tears, and they would never forget.

The Usher

Recently my husband and I attended the Nutcracker Ballet. The theater was crowded. There were people moving in every direction. We found ourselves being pushed and jostled upward as the stairway became increasingly steep and narrow. Unsure as to where we were going we looked around for an usher to direct us. Seeing our confusion, an attractive woman of sixty or so smiled and motioned for us to follow her as, flashlight in hand, she guided us safely down the balcony stairs and to our seats.

That same weekend, because of heavy snow and ice storms, many people were without electricity. A friend who lives in Michigan called to say that he and his wife would be staying in a hotel until further notice. No electricity means no light or heat. Pipes freeze. Telephone communication is cut off. And the little light that automatically switches on when you open the refrigerator door doesn't. A winter night without electricity can be very dark indeed.

"You are the light of the world" (Mt 5:14–16). Jesus doesn't say, "You will be the light of the world—some day." Or, "It would be nice if you would be the light of the world." He says, in no uncertain terms, "You *are* the light of the world." You are light in the darkness on a winter night. You are the flashlight in God's hand, guiding the confused traveler to safety. Your smile is the light that warms the heart of a child. Your humor is the light that eases a tense situation at the office. Your understanding is the light that lifts the burden of a woman concerned about an uncertain reading on an X-ray. Your patience is the light that reassures a nervous waitress on her first day on the job. You are the light that switches on when God opens the door.

But sharing our light takes time and effort. Are we willing to do what it takes to let our light shine before others? Or would we rather just pull a bushel basket over our head and continue to stumble around in the dark?

The Naval Supply Officer

A priest I know, who has been ordained over thirty years, says with some impatience that the Scriptures simply do not always connect to the world of work. Perhaps not, but there are many times when the connection rings clear as a bell.

There's an expression in corporate America about people "climbing the corporate ladder." It means doing whatever it takes to get to the top. What is implied is that, in order to be successful, you must continue the climb and never look back. If there's someone in your way you simply climb over them! Step on them if necessary. Peel their hands away from the rungs of the ladder. If they slip off into oblivion that just means less competition for you.

One young man I know joined the navy with the idea of making it a career. He received several promotions and was eventually put in charge of supplies for a fleet of submarines. In that capacity he realized that there was a great deal of waste and deal-making going on and he began reporting what he saw. As those involved saw their schemes being exposed and profits slipping away, they began to make life more and more difficult for him. He was shunned by some, and passed over for promotions. Eventually he left the military and entered the corporate sector. Again his reputation for honesty led to increasing amounts of responsibility.

However, with responsibility have come the inevitable jealousies. As he uncovers corporate dishonesty people who are profiting from the deals want to pull him down.

The wicked say, "Let us lie in wait for the righteous man, because he …reproaches us for sins against the law" (Wis 2:12). "Those conflicts and disputes among you, where do they come from?" (Jas 4:1). My friend the priest may be right. Perhaps there isn't always a connection between Scripture and work. But I'm not convinced. The Word of God is living and active and I believe that these words are as immediate today as they were the first time they were spoken, especially if you're the one in the way on someone else's corporate ladder!

The Attorney

It was during a Scripture workshop, part of an ongoing series, that it happened. The gentleman in question was a "regular." Bright and articulate, in-house counsel for a major investment firm, he rarely spoke. But when he did we knew he had given much thought to what he was about to say. The gospel was about our call to serve and follow Jesus. Talk turned to what "let them deny themselves" (Mt 16:24) might mean. And that's when he spoke. He only said three words, but they hung heavy in the air. "This is hard."

Jesus says that those who follow him "do not belong to the world" (Jn 17:14). What is this "world" the Scriptures are talking about? If it's only, as the newspapers would have us believe, a place of pain and violence where crime and terrorism run rampant and anything can be bought for a price, then it is most certainly not a world we would want to belong to anyway. This is the world we are called out of—called to create a better one.

Lawyers working for justice; healthcare professionals committed to tending broken spirits as well as broken bodies; financial agents creating opportunities to include all segments of our population and not just the privileged few; educators inviting children to their full potential. On and on we talked and slowly a new vision of "a new heaven and a new earth" (Rev 21:1), the world as God intends it, began to emerge.

We are called to see the world with new eyes, to build up the kingdom. We are called to stand up for what we believe, even when it seems like everyone in our world is against us. We are called to decide what kind of world we wish to belong to. It can be a lonely task, and Jesus never said it would be easy.

The Salesman

"And your Father who sees in secret will reward you" (Mt 6:6). Tony was a businessman. He owned a successful men's clothing store in an upscale area of town. But he was rarely there. You see, Tony was also a member of the Town Council, and whenever there was a problem to be solved he was the first one they called. Not the kind of problems that make the evening news, mind you. No, it was the little problems, like the family whose home had burned and who needed a place to live. Or the man who lost his job and needed an office where he could carry on a job search. Or the Lions' Club candy sale. Or the Knights of Columbus' Shop 'n' Share Days. It seemed that whenever someone had a need they called Tony.

Tony was active in his parish, too. Every year he headed the planning committee for the parish picnic. He knew whom to talk to about having a temporary stage and sound system set up. He knew the fire chief and whom to ask for help when you wanted to set up a barbecue grill to cook two- or three-hundred burgers and brats. And he knew how to cook them so that just the smell alone would make your mouth water.

Funny thing, though. The family in temporary housing never knew who had made the referral. And the man looking for work never knew that it wasn't just a coincidence when he got that great lead. Funny thing that the sixth-grade class got credit for the most candy sales ever and they never guessed why so many people just happened to stop by their booth. Funny thing that it just so happened that the picnic committee needed supplies the same week the Knights needed funds for a school gym in an inner city school. Funny thing that no one ever figured out that Tony wasn't out playing golf when he was away from his business.

Yes, Tony seemed to be everywhere, and nowhere. In fact, most of the people he helped never even knew Tony's last name. Funny thing…

The Publisher

Sometimes people say, "If I only worked for the church, then it would be easy for me to be a witness to the gospel." Or we hear, "If only Jesus still walked the earth, then it would be easy to follow him." But most of us don't work for the Church (and, if we're honest, those of us who do would have to argue the premise), and Jesus of Nazareth no longer walks as a sign among us.

Or does he? One gentleman, a retired publishing executive, wrote recently about his employees who, without even knowing they were doing it, demonstrated to him what it meant to witness to the gospel in the workplace. He was engaged in the painful process of splitting up the department's share of year-end bonus monies among eight team leaders. Unbeknownst to one another, two of the team leaders came into the executive's office and offered to forgo their year-end bonuses in favor of a third person, a man who they believed, while the least well-paid of the group, most deserved a generous bonus. They pointed out the disproportionate amount of stress and demands that had been made upon him during a year of reorganization; his increasing family obligations; the probability that he had been previously underpaid in the department from which he had come; and, most importantly, the value of his humor, stories, and laughter to other members of the team.

For the department head these two people were a sign of the gospel in the marketplace, as the third man was a sign to them all. Only later would the executive realize that, in his striving to remain aware of the presence of the holy, his own actions and beliefs were also a sign to others.

Jesus has been taken up into heaven. The power of the Holy Spirit has been poured out upon us. We are to be his witnesses. We are to be a Sign to the world in which we live. Why, then, are we standing here looking up at the sky (Lk 24:50–53)?

The Customer Service Representative

"Customer Service." We've all seen the sign. It might be in our favorite department store or car repair shop. "Customer service" might even determine which department store or car repair shop *is* our favorite! It's often the topic of articles in professional journals or one of the workshop offerings at trade shows. Obviously, given all the attention we pay to the subject, it must be important, but have you ever wondered why?

Some of the more obvious reasons might include "return business" and "word of mouth advertising," "product identification" and "corporate pride." Rarely, however, do we hear "because it's the right thing to do" or "respect for human dignity demands it." In fact, it could be very difficult to even introduce this kind of reasoning into the conversation. The business world understands dollars and cents (and the need for a place "to rest [one's] head"; Lk 9:58). Unfortunately, the business world too often fails to recognize the dignity of the paying customer. Sometimes, in business as elsewhere, we do the right thing for the wrong reason.

In Luke's gospel we encounter people who say they want to follow Jesus but who hesitate (9:59–62). They have other things to do first, business to take care of at home that must take priority. Jesus refuses to accept their excuses and, it would seem, leaves them behind.

Elisha also expressed a need to take care of business at home but, rather than reject him, Elijah waited (1 Kgs 19:19–21). What was different? Perhaps it was because Elisha's commitments had to do with loving service to others while the commitments referred to in Luke's gospel were self-serving. Elisha slaughtered twelve oxen (quite a large sacrifice!) to be given to the people for food. His reason for hesitating was already a response to Elijah's call to follow him. His "customer service" focused outward, reflecting love for family and service to others. The excuses in Luke's gospel focused inward, serving primarily the needs of those who hesitate. When Jesus calls us to offer "customer service" how do we respond? And why?

The Account Executive

"There was a man who had two sons..." (Lk 15:11).

It was Saturday morning. Joe woke early from a troubled sleep. He had spent most of the night tossing and turning. It was the morning after the awards banquet. He had been one of two finalists. He'd worked hard, even gone to workshops to improve his skills. He'd made it a point to be available for overtime, and he hardly ever took a day off. What were they thinking? How could they have given the award to Jim, of all people? Jim hadn't even finished high school. Oh, sure, he'd gone back for his GED, and he had even managed to get his college degree, but he'd only been working for the company for two years and he had practically no previous experience. What could they possibly have been thinking to give Jim the award instead of Joe?

The more Joe thought about it the more convinced he because that he had been wronged. "Probably someone's relative," he thought. Or, "they've passed me over because of my age." "Couldn't work his way out of a shoebox!" For the life of him he couldn't think of one good thing that Jim had done to win the award. He began watching him, hoping to catch him in some mistake. When Jim asked Joe for advice he would either make himself unavailable or pretend not to have the answer. He could tell that company a thing or two about their "award winner." They'd think twice before they passed him over again.

Meanwhile Jim, hardly able to believe his good fortune, worked harder than ever. He felt a little guilty about getting the award. He knew how hard Joe had worked for it. In fact, Joe had been a kind of role model for him.

The company president tried to talk to Joe, to tell him how much the company appreciated all that he had done over the years to contribute to its success. He tried to explain that Joe's salary was larger than that of any other employee and that he had been the first to benefit when they began offering stock options. He thanked him for his years of dedication and service. But Joe was hurt, and he refused to listen.

Probably Joe would never know that Jim was the one who had nominated him for the award in the first place.

The Director of Emergency Preparedness

It is October 2, 2001 as I write these words. Today, some five hundred people are working around the clock in the offices of the New York Emergency Preparedness Center—or, to be more precise, in a cruise ship terminal that has been converted to this use, their building having collapsed with the Twin Towers in New York City on September 11. One man is responsible for seeing that these people are supplied with all they need to conduct the business of rebuilding the city. A veteran of both police and fire departments, he lost many friends in the terrorist attack. But this is not the time for him to grieve. There is a job to be done; he will grieve later.

The head of this massive undertaking neither gives nor asks for special favors. He is simply grateful that he is alive and has the knowledge and skill to do what must be done. He tirelessly directs operations providing food, medical supplies, psychological support, even garbage removal. The people who work for him don't expect any recognition for what they do, either. It's their job and they do it. They respect the expertise of their director and act quickly to carry out his directives. It's a difficult job but they know that this is what they are obliged to do.

There is a passage from Luke's gospel (17:5–10) that relates to this situation. At first reading Luke's account might seem harsh, with words like "slave" and "worthless." But while the language may seem archaic the servant's attitude is not unlike that of the employees at the Emergency Preparedness Center. Their director trusts that they know what they have to do and that they will continue to do it, without expecting recognition or gratitude. Each will do what he or she is "obliged to do." In fact, looked at in this way, it seems that the master actually has faith in the servant, rather than the other way around.

The apostles asked Jesus to increase their faith. Jesus responded with a story that seemed to say that perhaps it is not the faith that is missing but rather the desire to live up to the expectations that the gift of faith places upon us...

The Reporter

There seems to be a need in the human heart to play "gotcha." It's not necessarily a bad thing. In fact, it's a technique often employed by trial lawyers and journalists. But it becomes destructive when the question is manipulated to destroy someone's reputation and/or credibility.

Sometimes the questioner will use this technique to make it appear that the one being questioned doesn't really know what he or she is talking about or, worse, agrees with a statement that is, in fact, contrary to what he or she really believes. Politicians are especially vulnerable to this kind of attack. In an electronic age it is relatively easy to manipulate sound bites, and in print the meaning of a statement can change drastically when it is taken out of context. "Do you still beat your wife? Just answer yes or no, please. Don't confuse me with the facts."

The Sadducees and the Pharisees used this tactic well. We see it often in the Scriptures. "[W]hose wife will the woman be?" (Lk 20:33); "Is it lawful to cure on the Sabbath?" (Mt 12:10); "Is it lawful for us to pay taxes to the emperor, or not?" (Lk 20:22). The question is intended to result in Jesus incriminating Himself. But the Sadducees and the Pharisees weren't the only ones who knew how to play this game. Sometimes we're pretty good at it ourselves.

It may be unintentional, a question tossed out without thinking, but most often the questioner knows exactly what he is doing, even to rehearsing the question over and over in his head. Since this particular form of attack works best when there is an audience present, the questioner may choose to pose his question at a press conference or public meeting. On the other hand, when a face-to-face encounter is impossible (or when the questioner wishes to avoid such an encounter), the Letters to the Editor column can work equally well. Either way, the objective is to insure that anything the one under attack says in response can and will be held against him.

Do our questions encourage others to think and speak their truth? Or do we, like the Sadducees, fashion our questions around the barb of self-incrimination?

The Insurance Adjuster

Meghan works as a claims adjuster for a major insurance company, but she's thinking of making a career change. She has been with the company for about ten years and is very good at what she does. She enjoys her work, or at least she did until recently. But things are changing. Today, even if a customer pays his or her insurance premium faithfully, more often than not the company cancels the policy when a claim is made on it. For Meghan it is becoming increasingly difficult to have to tell a family that has lost its home in a fire, or an individual diagnosed with a serious illness, that their insurance policies are being cancelled, especially when she knows that the same conditions for which they are making such claims may preclude them from getting insurance elsewhere.

Meghan is a caring person. She is the kind of person you want beside you when your world comes crashing in around you. Meghan gives people hope. After talking with her, customers feel less confused, less afraid. They know that, if anyone can cut through the red tape and help them retain their insurance coverage, it's Meghan. Unfortunately, the more her customers praise her, the more her supervisor goes out of his way to make her life difficult. Company policy is not on her side.

In the lectionary readings found at the end of the liturgical year, Scripture paints a picture of a world in chaos. "Lo, the day is coming…" (Mal 3:19-20). "Nation will rise against nation…" (Lk 21:5-19). In reality, however, these readings are about hope. It isn't easy to fight your way through the red tape involved in an insurance claim. It requires perseverance. None of us knows when disaster will strike, so we take out insurance policies in the hope that, should misfortune hit, we will survive. Meghan is working very hard to make that happen. But the system is beating her down, and Meghan is tired.

What do we do when negative forces gather against us? The answer, I believe, lies in another question: Who is *our* insurer?

The Accountant

Overheard at a meeting recently: "I just never thought that accounting would involve anything unethical." The young lady who was speaking had recently graduated from business school; she was one of the best and the brightest. Subsequently she had been recruited by a large accounting firm and taken a position with a very attractive salary. Unfortunately, she quickly learned just how unethical some business professionals could be when there was money to be made.

The woman was young. It was her first venture into the world of commerce. There were things going on that hadn't been covered in her college coursework. She was being asked to do "what worked," instead of what was right. But wasn't that what everyone else was doing?

The first time something had come up that didn't feel quite right she had tried talking to some of the other people in the firm, but they had only laughed and shaken their heads. On another occasion she went to her supervisor. The response there was even less supportive. She was told that it was her job to "get it done," by whatever means necessary. The company wasn't paying her to make decisions but only to follow through on decisions made by others. Even if, as she suspected, the decisions they were making were wrong, to refuse to do what was being asked of her could very possibly result in her dismissal.

She believed in God. But God didn't work at her firm. Not only that, God didn't even have a key to the front door! She felt very much alone. How could God ask her to risk everything she had worked for? Was taking an ethical stance worth losing her job? By whose standards should she judge—God's...or man's (Mt 16:21–27)?

It isn't easy to think as God thinks. It's far more comfortable thinking as human beings do. It seems so much easier just to "go along." After all, it could mean a six-figure salary. It's not like she's actually going to "forfeit her life" (Mt 16:26) or anything...

The Banker

Ordinary people doing ordinary work. A banker making a loan so that a young couple can build the home they've always dreamed about. A doctor listening intently to an elderly patient who lives alone. A butcher cutting meat; an accountant working with a client; a mechanic rebuilding an engine; a lawyer researching a case. People going about their ordinary work.

In Luke's gospel we hear about two fishermen who "have worked all night long but have caught nothing" (5:5). In Isaiah we read about a man "I am a man of unclean lips, and I live among a people of unclean lips" (Isa 6:5). And in Paul's letter to the Corinthians he describes himself as one who has "worked harder than any of them" (1Cor 15:10).

What could they possibly have in common? The answer, I believe, is *work*. But not *only* work. Rather, it is the ability, or inability, of each of these people to recognize God in their work. It is the ability to accept that we are not perfect but that God uses the imperfect to build up the kingdom. It is the willingness to become the instrument of grace while at the same time admitting our own need for God's grace in our lives.

The gift of Peter's work was that the people were fed. The gift of Paul's work was that the word was preached. The gift of the banker's work is that a young couple is able to build a home for their family. The butcher's work feeds the hungry. The doctor's work heals the sick. The accountant's work brings order out of financial chaos. The work of the mechanic may even save someone's life. Whether fisherman or banker, each of us has some work to do in building up the kingdom. But sometimes, in our sinfulness, we forget our need for God. We think that we are strong enough, or smart enough, or "whatever" enough, and we try to row out into the deep water alone. God is always present, but it's up to us to invite him to join us in the boat.

CHAPTER 2

Social Justice?
Or Just "Social"?

As I sit looking out
through tinted glass
upon the woodlands
on my way,

I see the panic in
the eyes of yellow children,
beaten bloody by
the soldiers in the streets.

As I ride on and listen
to the hum of wheels
on tracks laid firm
and straight,

I hear the screams
of travelers trapped
behind a wall
of flaming pain and death.

As I reflect upon
the many restaurants
we pass
along the way,

I hear the muffled cries
of babies sucking sadly—
nursing nipples
sapped of life.

As I look through the glass,
my God, I seek—
but cannot find—
your face.

As I recall
red silos full of grain—
they call to mind
those other silos filled with death.

And as I pull into my driveway,
garage so full of boxes
not one more
will fit,

I see the pleading faces
of a family of twelve
who'd gladly live there
and not have me move a thing.

How do I balance out
your love for me
against the tens of thousands
crying in their sleep tonight?

I seek an answer, God!

I call on you,
O Mighty God
of love and peace—
Reveal yourself!

And show to me the answers
to the puzzles passing by
as I look out through tinted glass
upon my way.

It was 6:00 in the evening and I was on the train, headed for my home in the suburbs west of Chicago. Perhaps it was the steady hum of the wheels, or maybe I was just tired, but as I watched the city slowly falling away and being replaced by suburb after suburb, these words began to take shape in my head. The newspapers—then as now—were full of war and rumors of war. The graphic images I had seen over and over on the evening news rose up and took shape before my eyes, and it was as if I was watching some kind of macabre newsreel playing outside the train window.

Citizens were being beaten in the streets in Asia. A train wreck in South Africa killed dozens as would-be rescuers stood by helpless before a wall of flames fed by the train's cargo of fuel oil. Fast-food restaurants and trendy cafes in the passing landscape offered everything from hamburgers for a dollar to coffee for five, while in my mind's eye I saw the emaciated faces of children starving in the streets of third world countries, their mothers helpless, themselves too malnourished to offer more than a dry breast to calm their babies' cries.

There is a farm on the way, with an old house that was once white and outbuildings faded by years of sun and neglect. Something about the silo seemed vaguely familiar. And then I remembered another landscape, and other silos—but they were not filled with grain.

Later, having left the train for my car and the last few miles of my commute home, I touched the button on my automatic garage door opener and watched the door slide silently upwards. What greeted me was a pile of cardboard boxes, many still unpacked even though we had moved into this house almost two years earlier. I thought of people who were being displaced in my own city as neighborhoods became more gentrified and less accessible to the poor. And I thought of people who *lived* in cardboard boxes.

I began to pray the scene that passed behind my eyelids. I still do not know the answer to my question. Why am I here, in this land of sun and plenty, while others huddle in darkness and want? It is a question that haunts me. But while I may never know the answer this side of the kingdom, I am convinced that it is a question I must never stop asking.

Clothe the Naked

The story is told of a New Orleans philanthropist, known for her generosity to hospitals and other charities. One December day, sitting in her living room, she came across a cartoon in a magazine. The cartoon pictured two ragged street women shivering over a small fire. One turned to the other and asked what she was thinking about. "I'm thinking about all the nice, warm clothes the rich ladies will give us next summer." The story goes on to tell how the woman immediately dropped the magazine, went up to her attic, searched through boxes and trunks, and made up bundles of warm clothing to be distributed the very next day (Mt 25:36).

A good story, and a good lesson—but what about us? Have we gone up to the attic lately? Or do we spend our lives sitting in our living rooms, planning what good things we will do "someday" for "someone" while ignoring the needs of the people closest to us? Are we able to get outside ourselves and our own little worlds, or are we so blind to the people we live and work with that we no longer see that they have needs today? Do we plan to visit the children's ward at the hospital next week but neglect to visit the attic where we have stored a warm concern about public policy regarding a possible cutback in hospital funding which could impact not only hospital patients but employees and their families as well? Do we volunteer for the suicide hotline but neglect to visit the attic where we have stored our ability to listen when a fellow employee needs to talk to someone about a hospital test that came back positive?

And what about our families? I know one secretary who can tell by the tone of her boss's voice if he is talking to a client or to his wife. Does the tone of our voice speak louder than our words? Are we kinder to strangers than to those with whom we live? Do we smile and speak kindly to clients but neglect to visit the attic where we have stored a warm heart for those we live with and love?

There is a folk song that was popular several years ago. Its text was taken from the Old Testament book of Ecclesiastes: "For everything there is a season, and a time for every matter under heaven..." (3:1–8). Now is the time, and this is the season. Who are the "street people" in our lives, waiting this winter day for the warm clothes we have stored in our attics?

Shelter the Homeless

Jesus reminds his followers that whoever wishes to be great must be willing to serve (Mk 10:42–45). In her book, *My Grandfather's Blessings*, Rachel Naomi Remen says, "True service…is a relationship between people who bring the full resources of their combined humanity to the table and share them generously." She goes on to explain that serving is not the same as helping. "When we help we become aware of our strength…but we do not serve with our strength; we serve with ourselves." The disciples sought to rule with power and authority. Jesus sought only to serve out of his humanity.

Several years ago as part of a class I was teaching at Mundelein Seminary I showed my students a clip from the movie, *Entertaining Angels*, the life story of Dorothy Day. The action takes place after Day, having undergone a series of conversion experiences, has founded the Catholic Worker House where she serves and cares for the homeless poor of New York City. The cardinal comes to her house and explains, rather apologetically, that her work of service is "embarrassing" to the Church. He then asks her to remove the word "Catholic" from their name. Dorothy's reply? "But we *are* Catholic."

The Catholic Worker movement did not begin in a monastery. Nor was it carried out in a church building. Dorothy Day and those who worked with her chose to serve the poor out of their own humanity in their own time and place. They chose to drink the cup of human suffering, as Jesus did (Mk 10:38–39). They did not *help* the poor; they *served* them. They fought for human dignity and the right of the individual to decent living and working conditions and a just wage.

Dorothy Day did not claim any authority in her own right. Rather, she claimed only her weakness. But in her weakness was her strength. Are we strong enough to claim our weakness? Are we willing to serve others in our own time and place?

Feed the Hungry

Perhaps because so many of us at some time or another find life's stresses almost overwhelming, the expression "sweating blood," taken from Luke's gospel (22:44), has become a familiar part of our language. Thanks to William Shakespeare we talk about paying a debt with "a pound of flesh." And many of us remember singing "a poor man is made out of muscle and blood." Our language is rich with such expressions. Yes, we are spiritual beings, but we also have bodies. That's how God made us.

God made us with bodies that get hungry and thirsty, tired and cold. So we work. We "sweat blood" for a paycheck, pouring out everything we have to complete a project or meet a deadline. Computers multiply on our desks and in our pockets, tethering us by their mouse-tail umbilical cords. We work long hours to feed our bodies, only to find that our spirits are starving. New books on spirituality multiply overnight on bookstore shelves. But none of it is enough. Like the crowd in Luke's gospel (9:11–17), we are hungry.

In June we celebrate the feast of the Body and Blood of Christ. We hear stories about hungry people and stories of bread and fish that miraculously appear and satisfy the multitude. We hear stories about people whose spirits are starving and stories of bread and wine that are shared and poured out to feed their souls. We hear stories of people who are not us, and yet, who are. People who are hungry.

We profess in our Creed that Christ sits "at the right hand of the Father." Where, precisely, is that? Well, if God is everywhere, then Christ must be everywhere too, right? And if Christ is everywhere, then the Body and Blood of Christ must be present wherever people are "sweating blood" to make ends meet, wherever people are hungry for meaning or starving for dignity. Where is the Body of Christ? We are the Body of Christ! The Body of Christ is right here. The multitude is waiting to be fed. Jesus is speaking to us. "You give them something to eat" (Lk 9:13).

Visit the Imprisoned

A friend recently sent me a copy of an article describing *pro bono publico* (Latin for "the public good or welfare"—when attorneys take on cases without compensation to advance a social cause they are said to be representing the party *pro bono publico* or *pro bono*) services being provided by over fifteen thousand attorneys around Chicago. Examples include everything from working to obtain asylum for immigrants, providing low-cost and no-cost legal services around issues including housing, consumer fraud, domestic relations, and child abuse to organizing charity fundraisers and implementing programs to remove gang graffiti.

Although the work may not be specifically "religious," it clearly revolves around protecting the human dignity of the individual, a key component of Catholic social teaching. This work is not being done in the Church; rather, it is being done for the church and by the church, that is, the people of God.

In a reading from the prophet Isaiah we see how Cyrus was used by God (45:1-5, 9-11). Cyrus was a Gentile king yet Isaiah refers to him as "God's anointed one." Did Cyrus consider himself God's agent? Probably not. Do these attorneys consider themselves God's agents? Probably not. But just as God used Cyrus to bring the Jews back from the Babylonian exile God uses these attorneys to bring God's people back from the exile of substandard housing, domestic abuse and violence.

While these women and men spend much of their time and talent earning their living and paying their taxes, they also choose to "give back" something of the considerable power, skill, and ability entrusted to them—or, as we might say in religious language, to "give therefore to the emperor the things that are the emperor's, and to God the things that are God's" (Mt 22:21).

Honor the Dignity of Others

While by no means limited to these topics, Catholic social thought takes special note of human dignity and the principle of subsidiarity. The dignity of the human person, simply defined, means that every man and every woman is created in the image of God and deserves to be treated with respect. God has breathed God's own Spirit into each one of us. We are temples of the Holy Spirit, tabernacles of the Body of Christ, and we must treat one another accordingly. The principle of subsidiarity holds that problems are, as far as possible, to be resolved at the level closest to those involved. People deserve to have some control over their lives and the conditions under which they live and work.

The Scriptures reflect similar concerns. The writer of Proverbs praises the "capable wife" for the dignity she brings to her work and for the good use to which she puts her God-given talents (31:10–13, 19–20, 30–31). She does not look to others to do for her what she can do for herself, and the author of Proverbs assures the reader that the woman will be rewarded for her labors.

The three servants in Matthew's gospel (25:14–30) also possess talents, given to them by their master. Two of them use their talents wisely, bringing about increased growth and development of their gifts. The third servant, however, hides his talents and in so doing deprives himself and those around him of the benefits his gifts are meant to provide. He denies his human potential and his very dignity as a thinking, functioning human person.

Do we recognize or deny the dignity of those with whom we live and work? Do we encourage others to use their talents? Do we mentor those less skilled than ourselves, sharing what we know and praising them when they are successful? Or are we jealous of the abilities of friends and co-workers, afraid of their accomplishments? Are we children of the light, rejoicing in the giftedness of people around us? Or do we prefer the darkness of talents buried under layers of selfishness, criticism, and lost opportunities? When the day of the Lord arrives will the Master find us alert to our human dignity, or asleep with an unopened gift box in our lap?

Defend the Widow

We've all heard the saying, "the more things change the more they stay the same." A reading from Luke's gospel seems to bear this out. The people of Capernaum were looking for a powerful Messiah. Instead they heard Jesus, their relative (raised up from among their own kin), teaching with authority and casting out unclean spirits (Lk 4:21–30).

We know from other gospel passages how difficult it was for the people in Jesus' hometown to accept that "Joseph's son" could work signs and wonders (Lk 4:22). They were looking for something out of the ordinary. Because they did not understand how he was able to speak with such authority, they did not recognize him. Oddly enough, however, the unclean spirit *did* recognize him (Lk 4:34)! The unclean spirit knew God's voice, and rejected it.

We might wonder why, with so much evidence in his favor, the people of Jesus' time had such difficulty in knowing him. But are we doing any better? Every four years we embark on another presidential marathon. Candidates crisscross the country, speaking wherever they can find an audience. They know that as long as they say what we want to hear—whether about taxes, the economy, spending policies, whatever—they will be accepted. Most do not choose to challenge the status quo. But what about those who speak out with authority on behalf of the poor, the dispossessed, the marginalized? More often than not, they are rejected.

God is still present in the world. In ordinary people and in ordinary ways God speaks with authority. But too often we choose to reject God's voice. Could it be that, like that unclean spirit, we choose to reject God's presence in the ordinariness of life because the cost of doing otherwise would be more than we're willing to pay?

Hear the Orphan's Plea

Given the increasing awareness of unacceptable working conditions around the world several major universities are currently reexamining the manufacturers with whom they contract for production of sportswear, sporting equipment, and other signature items. Decent working conditions and just salary levels are becoming the standards for choosing producers and suppliers. There is a concerted effort being made to release workers in substandard facilities from the paralyzing conditions imposed upon them by our desire to acquire cheaply made items. Our sin of greed has corrupted the economic systems in many third world countries. Now, it seems, we must ask forgiveness for our sins.

Americans are good at forgiving the sins of others. Many times we have helped countries that were once our enemies to rebuild their cities. We have poured hundreds of thousands of dollars into faltering economies when countries have found themselves torn by internal strife. And these are very good things. But we are not always quite so good at *asking* for forgiveness. It is very difficult for us to admit it when we are wrong. We would rather write a check and go on about our business.

Perhaps that's why it is so refreshing to see universities acting for justice.

In an economy that is driven by "demand" we often turn a blind eye to what goes on in the area of "supply." True, some retailers have taken a stand in this regard, but usually only when their sales were threatened by customers who demanded they do so. In the case of the universities, however, sales were just fine. Rather, it was the students themselves who, because of a growing and genuine concern over our sins against workers on the other side of the globe, broke a hole through the ceiling of the marketplace and asked for healing for workers who were themselves too paralyzed by the system in which they were caught to act on their own behalf (Mk 2:3–5).

On whose behalf am I called to act? For what sins must I ask forgiveness?

Comfort the Afflicted

Three words basic to the development of Catholic social teachings are *see*, *judge*, and *act*. First, we are called to *see*, to take notice of and pay attention to what is going on around us. While, for our purposes, we will apply this to the workplace, it can as easily apply to home, school, neighborhood, community, parish, and so on. Next, after taking the time to look closely at what is at issue, we think about the situation, and *judge* its ramifications, not based only on its merits but in light of gospel values and the traditions and teachings of the Church. Only then are we called to *act* (we often try to get to this step first, without going through the first two).

In John's gospel (14:1–12), Thomas asks, "how can we know the way?" ("How do we know what action to take?") Jesus responds in frustration to a questions asked by Philip, "Have I been with you all this time…and you still do not know me?" He almost seems to say, "Haven't you been able to figure it out yet?" We read this and wonder why the apostles, who saw and walked with Jesus, just couldn't seem to "get it."

But "getting it" isn't just about seeing. It also requires judgment. We must first think about what we see and what it means. Then, and only then, are we called to act: "whoever believes in me will *do* the works that I do." In Acts (6:1–6) we read that some of the disciples "complained…because their widows were being neglected" (see). The twelve "called together the whole community" to look at the situation in light of their new understanding in faith (judge). Then they appointed men to the task (act).

Jesus was frustrated with the apostles because they just didn't seem to "get it." If he were to walk into our homes and workplaces today would he see anything that would make him feel any differently about us?

Encourage the Lost

"What are you looking for?"

As the opening line in a television commercial this question is answered by advertisers before we've even had time to realize it has been asked. A new car, a vacation cruise, fashion jeans, faster computers, designer water—on and on. Our consumer society *tells* us what we're looking for.

But Jesus *asks*, "What are you looking for?" (Jn 1:38). Then he waits for an answer. The response of the disciples seems strange. Rather than answering, they ask a question of their own: "where are you staying?" In other words, "What are you really about? What makes you tick?"

Perhaps, before we spend our entire life working for what we think we want—money, power, prestige, the top rung of the corporate ladder—we need to take some time to ask ourselves what we're looking for. Like Samuel, we need to verify who it is that calls us. Do we respond to the voice of the economy, regardless of what effect it may have on our family? what impact it may have on the environment? what cost to workers in terms of justice and human dignity?

Stephen R. Covey puts it this way: "I had finally reached the top of the ladder when I realized it was up against the wrong wall!" Catholic social teaching demands that we check out the wall before we put up our ladder. The apostles asked, "where are you staying?" "Come and see" was Jesus' answer (Jn 1:39). They responded to his invitation, and what they saw changed them forever—so much so, in fact, that not only did they decide to stay with Jesus but they invited others to join them.

If someone we live or work with asks, "Where are you staying?" ("What are you really about?"), can we invite them to "come and see"? If not, it may be that we, like the disciples, need to stop and ask ourselves just what it is we're really looking for…

Shelter the Homeless

There is, in Catholic social teaching, something called the "principle of subsidiarity," which means handling a problem at the level closest to it. In Mark's gospel a leper approaches Jesus who, "moved with pity," *touches* and cures him (Mk 1:40–45). Jesus doesn't avoid the encounter by telling the man to go see a doctor. Jesus handles the problem at the immediate level. He touches the man that everyone else avoids.

But Jesus doesn't act in a vacuum. He sends the man to the priest so that the legal requirements for his return to society might be met. Rather than circumventing the law, Jesus shows respect for it, but only after he has done what he can do for the man.

Jesus instructs the man *not* to tell anyone what has happened. Jesus isn't looking for publicity. His action is driven by compassion, not by political ambition. Later Paul will instruct the Corinthians similarly to "do everything for the glory of God." The message is clear.

Right now there is a great deal in the news about "affordable housing." As older neighborhoods become gentrified many of the present inhabitants are, in effect, told to "dwell apart," to make their abode "outside the camp." The poor become the homeless; the homeless become the leper. While current employment statistics generally include day laborers as "full-time" workers the fact is that many of these people, due to the lack of affordable housing, are homeless. Politicians make promises. It makes good press.

Mark tells us that Jesus was "moved with pity." Acting within the norms of the law and society in which He lives, Jesus makes it possible for the man to regain his full human dignity. Our newspapers are full of similar stories, but more often than not we look the other way and assume that "they"—the government, social service agencies, politicians, whoever "they" happen to be in the present situation—will handle it.

Advertisements for phone companies and teleflorists urge us to "reach out and touch someone." And that may not be a bad idea. After all, isn't that what Jesus did?

Redress the Wronged

Back in the early 1980s I became involved in youth ministry, convinced that for young people to develop strong Christian values it is important that they feel supported. Taking the gospel seriously is not easy. Making choices based on an informed conscience rather than on what's profitable can make one unpopular. Our hope was that as these teens grew into adulthood they would have the courage to stand up for what they believed was right.

Unfortunately, upon entering the work force many of us find ourselves faced with conflicting values. Increased salary often means increased hours away from home and family. Increased power may require a lessening of concern for employees' rights and needs. Decisions that oppose an informed conscience become easier to make when the corporate culture supports the outcome and cares little for how it is achieved.

Catholic social teaching has long held that people have the right to join a union, provided that the purpose of the union is to protect the basic rights and dignity of the worker. While a single person speaking out on an issue may be looked upon as "radical" or "dangerous," a group of workers speaking out for justice has a better chance of making its voice heard.

The assembly line worker who stands up and says "Enough!" may face dismissal for her position. A black woman sitting down on a bus in a seat reserved for whites, a young woman in New York City demanding to know why workers were not being paid a living wage, a machinist lodging a complaint about unsafe working conditions only to have the paperwork mysteriously disappear—each of these people was a prophet in his own time and place (Lk 40:4–24). Each faced anger and the threat of being ostracized by the community.

Remember the story on page 12, about the young attorney at a Bible study? His words about doing what is necessary if we are to take the gospel seriously are worth repeating: "This is really hard."

Welcome the Stranger

There is something exciting happening at fast food restaurants, or maybe I'm just the last to notice. While fast food has always offered a good job opportunity for high school students and adults with entry-level skills, there seems to be a growing trend toward hiring persons with physical and/or mental disabilities.

The first time I noticed this was in a restaurant near my office. There was something distinctive about the young man sweeping the floor, a combination of characteristics common in individuals with Down Syndrome. But there was something more; there was a genuine desire to be of service. As I looked around for an empty table he smiled and, broom in hand, said, "That table over there is clean. You can sit there, if you want." Then he went on about his work of sweeping the floor.

And sweep it he did! That young man swept the floor like no floor has ever been swept before. He actually seemed to enjoy sweeping the floor. It was obvious that he took great pride in his work. But each time someone entered the restaurant he would stop what he was doing, smile broadly at the newcomer and, with as much grace as if he was welcoming them into his own home, direct them to a clean table.

In the aftermath of September 11, 2001, we are more grateful than ever for our rights and freedoms, one being the right to expect a just wage for our labor. Yet many of the most vulnerable among us are still held captive. For the young man in the fast food restaurant the availability of an entry-level job offers freedom from the captivity of people's prejudices and fears and the independence to live his life with dignity and respect. For me, his presence is a reminder that what is "hidden…from the wise and the learned" truly is revealed to us through the "little ones." "Come to me, all you who labor" (Mt 11:25–30).

Are we as grateful as the young man in the fast food restaurant is for the independence we enjoy?

CHAPTER 3

Stereotypes
(Who *Really* Goes There?)

She sits so peacefully
'mid rush hour travelers—
sleeping child
upon her breast.

Hair, hidden by the veil
worn in Eastern lands
from times long past.

A smile plays across her face
and dances in her eyes.

I smile back...
a mother's smile...
shared across the ages.

I understand
her mother's heart,
even though her words
are in a language
lost to me.

Her olive skin...
her eyes so dark...
her youthful beauty
and serenity.

So must the mother
of my infant king
have looked
that ancient night...
sitting peacefully
'mid rush hour travelers
on their way
to Bethlehem.

I was riding home on the subway. It had been a long day. The train was crowded with rush hour commuters and by the time I got on there was not a seat to be had, so I ended up standing, wedged in between what seemed like hundreds of other tired people. That was when I saw her.

She was sitting in the window seat nearest to where I was standing. There was a child on her lap—a boy, probably not even a year old—and our eyes met when she caught me looking down at the two of them. That's when we smiled.

Now, as any mother knows, there are some bonds that reach beyond cultural differences, and motherhood is probably near the top of the list. It's nearly impossible for anyone who has ever carried and birthed a child not to connect with another woman who has shared that experience. When our eyes met there was an instant recognition and identification. It was as though we had known one another for a very long time—and perhaps we had.

With some surprise it occurred to me that this young woman was probably dressed very much as Mary would have been, given that she was from the same part of the world. And I wondered if this might not be how Mary would have looked, had she been traveling on a subway train in Chicago instead of on a donkey in Bethlehem...

Church People

I had recently left my job in a downtown office. Midlife career change, some people might call it. Now I found myself, for the first time, working full-time for the Church. It was a dream come true in almost every way. But one day, shortly after having taken the position, I had an experience that, while it probably shouldn't have surprised me, did.

I won't bore you with details. Suffice it to say that I had what was, for me, a deeply spiritual experience. It was so powerful that I felt I had to share it with someone—but there was no one there! Somehow I had expected that, in a parish situation, there would be someone with whom I could share a deeply spiritual experience! I even went so far as to call a priest friend of mine in another parish—but he was away at a funeral. I called a woman friend who does parish work—she was in a meeting. There was no one to tell! And I realized with startling clarity that, had I still been working at my previous job, I would have had several close friends who would have immediately understood.

How many of us have these fleeting moments, experiences of God, but no one with whom to share them? Something happens. Perhaps some prayer is answered, or isn't. Like the Samaritan woman at the well when she realized that the man with whom she was talking was indeed the Messiah (Jn 4:28–29), we want to shout to the world, "There is a God!"—but there's no one there to hear. It's hard to believe but maybe, just maybe, "being Church" has nothing at all to do with where we work…

Sales People

Have you ever walked into a room and had the distinct feeling that something was "off"? People seemed to be getting along but there was something about the situation that made you uncomfortable. Perhaps it was the lack of courtesy when the office manager spoke to her assistant, or the mechanic's rudeness when you brought your car in for service. Something wasn't right. Their actions spoke louder than their words.

Or, on the other hand, did you ever walk in expecting problems but ended up experiencing just the opposite? The image of the used car salesman comes to mind. Probably one of the most maligned professions (second, perhaps, only to lawyers), the used car salesman is usually described as someone who paints a pretty picture of a car in mint condition knowing full well that it's been in a major wreck. We're almost surprised when he or she deals with us honestly.

The truth is that we often see in others the very traits that we try to avoid seeing in ourselves. People around us become a kind of mirror reflecting both our virtues and our vices. Maybe we're suspicious of someone else's honesty because we know we haven't always been honest ourselves. When the store clerk rings up an item at more than its marked price we're quick to complain, but do we protest when the price charged is less than it should be? If I'm the one selling the used car do I claim it's in better shape than it actually is? Do I "forget" to mention that it's been in an accident, or that it drinks oil and guzzles gas? Maybe one reason lawyers become the target of so many bad jokes is that people hire them in an attempt to get out of taking responsibility for their own actions and then blame them for being successful.

It's easy for us to see the culpability of others. It's harder to see our own. But then, considering the size of the beam in our eye (Lk 6:41–42), it's sometimes a wonder that we can see anything at all...

Cleaning People

Irene was the lead housekeeper. It was her job to make sure that all twelve coffeepots on all twelve floors of the high-rise office building were kept clean and filled with fresh, hot coffee. She was good at her job. She was proud of the spotless coffeepots and clean cups waiting to be filled. It never seemed to bother her that, even though she was standing right there, the people in the offices hardly saw her. In fact, she had come to expect it.

When word started to circulate that the big shots were coming in from the home office everyone began organizing files and clearing away stacks of paper in anticipation of a surprise visit. The big day found everyone in their respective offices, looking busier than anyone could remember. Everyone, that is, except Irene. In fact, had anyone even thought about it, they would have realized that no one had seen Irene all morning. But even if they had taken the time to look they probably wouldn't have found her. Because Irene wasn't running from floor to floor making coffee; Irene was sitting in the large conference room chatting with the visitors from the home office!

The tiny woman that most people barely noticed had just finished setting out the silver coffee service, hoping to catch a glimpse of the people who were causing such a stir in the office, when the guests arrived. She was about to leave when the visitors, realizing that this was probably the only person in the office who wasn't trying to impress them, had insisted that Irene sit down and have a cup of coffee with them.

Most of the people in Luke's gospel probably didn't even notice Zacchaeus up there in that sycamore tree, trying to get a peek at Jesus (Lk 19:1–10). But Jesus saw him. Jesus saw them all. Jesus saw the people who believed they were better than Zacchaeus; and Jesus saw Zacchaeus, who knew himself to be a sinner.

What tree must I climb to see Jesus? And how will I respond if he invites me to join him for coffee?

Professional People

All day long financiers, lawyers, healthcare professionals, and clerical workers share the streets of the city with the unemployed and the home-less. Every day men and women—some well dressed, others carrying all that they own on their backs—visit the church. Some dash in and out on their way to work; others simply wander through, looking for a place to rest or to get warm. Harold and Anthony were two of those people.

Harold was a lawyer, the product of a prestigious law school. Every morning he attended the 8:00 AM Mass, sitting in the third pew from the front on Mary's side, a man of power and influence, dependent on no one. Across the aisle, in the third pew on St. Joseph's side, sat Anthony. Anthony, however, never stayed for only one Mass. In fact, he usually attended several, remaining in his pew well into the day because Anthony, unlike Harold, had no job to go to.

Two men, neither aware of the other, so different from one another that the four feet of center aisle that separated them could just as easily have been four miles. At least, that is, until one Friday morning in November. It was the day after Thanksgiving and the schools were closed. Rebecca and her seven-year-old son, Sam, had taken the early train into town. They decided to stop at a downtown church for a visit on their way to see Santa. Morning Mass was well in progress, and the priest was just beginning to say the Our Father as they entered. In his excitement Sam broke away from his mother, ran straight up the center aisle, and landed in the third pew on St. Joseph's side, right beside Anthony. Doing what he was used to doing in his home church, Sam reached up and took Anthony's hand. Then, before his mother could catch him, he stretched across the aisle and took Harold's hand as well.

"Two people went up to the temple to pray; one a [lawyer] and the other [lived on the streets]" (Lk 18:10–14). Two men whose lives might never have intersected, one powerful and the other powerless, brought together by the innocence of a child.

Old People

Every day like clockwork, at precisely 1:45 PM, the elderly woman dressed entirely in black would appear at the door of her attorney's office. "Is he in?" she would ask; and the secretary, knowing that her boss was in but that he had left specific instructions that he did not want to see this particular client, would politely respond that he was not. "Then I'll wait," she would reply. And the tiny woman would settle into one of the large leather chairs, where she would remain for the next two hours. Finally, just before 4:00 PM, she would rise and, with the weariness of years in her voice, inform the young woman that she was leaving but that she would be back.

The attorney wasn't especially worried about the problems of the old woman. He really didn't care if her tenants paid their rent or not, even if it meant that she was being treated unjustly. As long as she continued to pay his retainer fee he wasn't about to tell her to leave, but he wasn't going to waste any time listening to her problems, either. He was a busy man with political aspirations. He dined with the rich and the famous and no old woman was going to impose herself upon his calendar. But while he feared neither God nor man, truth be told, the old woman was starting to get on his nerves.

When we hear Luke's gospel (18:1–8) about the widow and the judge, we usually assume that the judge in the story represents God. But let's look at the story again, now played out in an oak-paneled law office. The attorney is supposed to uphold the law, to protect the poor and the powerless, yet we find him lying to avoid doing precisely that. Is this an image of God?

But if not the attorney, or the judge, then who? The only other choice, it seems, must be the widow! The widow, who waits patiently, demanding justice and refusing to turn her back on what is right. Could it be the widow who is to image God for us, and not the judge at all (Sir 35:12–20)?

Blind People

Several years ago I had the good fortune to visit the Holy Land. At one point, as we gathered to pray in the Garden of Olives, someone said, "Let's sing something." At first we couldn't come up with anything everyone knew. Then someone started singing "Amazing Grace" and soon everyone was singing along.

When I was growing up "Amazing Grace" was not sung in our Catholic churches. I don't remember how or when I first learned the words but I'm quite sure that the first time I found it in a Catholic hymnal was sometime after Vatican II. Yet there we were—three priests, five women religious and thirty-seven Catholic lay men and women—and the only song we all knew was this lovely old Protestant hymn. What had once separated now united, and there where Jesus, betrayed by the blindness of Judas, had prayed, we sang "Was blind but now I see."

Because he was blind, Bartimaeus was considered an outcast (Mk 10:46–52). Separated from society he was tolerated by some, ignored by most. But, in fact, the so-called "sighted" people around him were far more blind to his existence than he was to theirs. Seeing with the eyes of faith Bartimaeus was able to look beyond the artificial divisions their sight imposed on them.

Separation blinds us because it allows us to stop seeing those around us. When we separate ourselves based on differences in physical or mental ability we become blind to those who are physically or mentally challenged. When we separate ourselves based on differences in theology or ideology we become blind to those who worship or believe differently than we do. When we separate ourselves based on artificial criteria for what is or is not acceptable we become like blind beggars, begging for the gift of sight, yet refusing to see.

Jesus is calling each one of us. How do we respond? Do we spring up to follow him? Do we really want to see? Or do we prefer to continue sitting blindly by the side of the road?

Sick People

Two women, each considered "unclean" in the eyes of the world—two stories of faith.

The woman bleeding for twelve years did not give up but reached out in faith for healing (Mk 5:25–34). What must it have been like to be weak, perhaps in pain, reduced to poverty by the cost of seeking a cure, shunned by society? Perhaps she felt like a woman I knew who died recently after a prolonged battle with cancer. Another friend and I visited her shortly before her death. She, too, reached out to Jesus in faith, not for a cure but for healing. We prayed together and she shared with us how grateful she was for all the disease had taught her.

The second story is of a little girl (Mk 5:21–24, 35–43). Even as she was dying her father reached out in faith for healing. To touch a dead body was to become ritually unclean, but Jesus did not hesitate. And Scripture tells us that the child arose, walked, and, restored to health, was given something to eat. When have I felt deadened by life? Was it my own faith that brought me back or, like that little girl, did I depend on the faith of another? Have I ever stepped out in faith on behalf of someone else?

Jesus insisted that it was faith that had restored life and health. Society shunned the woman with the hemorrhage but she didn't give up. She trusted that if she could only touch his cloak, the grace of God flowing out from Jesus would make her whole. Society scoffed at Jairus but he believed and did what Jesus instructed. The power of their deep faith in Jesus brought the dead and the near-dead back from the margins of life. Do we reach out, even when it seems hopeless to do so? Do we advocate for those who have been marginalized and condemned to death? It takes courage to reach out in faith. Are we up to the challenge?

Foreign People

A Vietnamese priest was staying with us at the parish where I was working. He was traveling across the country, preaching on the Eucharist, and working to help rebuild the church in Vietnam—the Church, the Body of Christ—in a word, "us." We were eating lunch together in the rectory kitchen.

"We are very good," he said, "at believing that the bread and wine are truly changed into the Body and Blood of Christ at the Eucharist (Mk 14:22–24), and we are pretty good at believing that we are called to become the Body of Christ to one another when we receive communion. But," he continued, "what we have difficulty with is believing that, when we receive the Eucharist, we become one with every other member of the Body of Christ."

When I asked what he meant he went on to explain that most of us readily see our relationship with God in the vertical axis of the cross and our call to give ourselves to others in the horizontal. However, we are much less comfortable with the idea of receiving others into ourselves, thereby becoming one with the *entire* Body of Christ.

When I still didn't understand he continued, "The Body of Christ is made up of *everyone*, not just those people with whom we feel comfortable. When we say 'Amen' to becoming one with the Body of Christ we say 'Amen' to becoming one with everyone; with those people with whom we have been at war, as well as at peace; with people having different belief systems and political ideologies; with people who do not live as we live or think as we think. When we say 'Amen' to becoming one with the Body of Christ we say 'Amen' to becoming one with the entire people of God regardless of age, race, sexual orientation, national origin, physical capability, or mental acuity."

Some say that Jesus ate and drank with all the wrong people. Then he left, instructing us to go and do likewise. I learned a little more of what that meant while eating lunch with a Vietnamese priest who was staying with us at the rectory where I was working.

Ordinary People

"You are the Messiah, the Son of the living God" (Mt 16:13–17).

With these words Peter answers the crucial question regarding Jesus' identity. In a few simple words Jesus is identified as Messiah, God is identified as "the living God" of the Jews, and the relationship between Jesus and God is established. In asking the question Jesus reflects a need as old as humanity, the need to be known. By answering the question in a way that expresses relationship, Peter reveals not just an intellectual fact but a deeper, more intimate way of knowing.

We all share this very human need to be known, but there is something else we share, as well. Because we are all children of God each one of us can be rightfully known as "son or daughter of God." Carried to the next step, this means that we must recognize every person we encounter as son or daughter of God. This identity is common to us all at all times, whether at the Sign of Peace at Mass or across the conference table at the office.

This account of a deepening understanding of Jesus' identity is told in all three of the synoptic gospels (Matthew, Mark, and Luke). It marks a turning point both in how Jesus views himself and in how he is viewed by the apostles. Once he is recognized as "Son of God" everything changes. Jesus knows and is known in a new way, and the people around him relate to him differently.

How would we relate to the people we live and work with if we recognized each one of them as a son or daughter of God? How would we act toward the people around us if we recognized ourselves as sons or daughters of God? Each person we meet, whether at home or at work, asks the same, human question: "Who do you say that I am?" How do we respond?

Passionate People

It has been said that it can be very difficult to live with a prophet. Think about it. Have you ever known someone who is so totally focused on an issue that nothing else seems to matter? They can't seem to talk about anything else. And they have very little patience for anyone who isn't as focused as they are. It's as though their passion takes on a life of it own.

I once received a request from a local union organizer asking that I take a stand against allegedly unfair labor practices in one area of our city. The request had been sent out to many church personnel in the area, but there had been little response. The organizer couldn't understand the resounding silence in response to her request for support. Given the issues as they were set forth there would seem to be no question that local churches would want to support the workers, but few seemed to want to get involved.

Why is the message of this organizer so difficult to hear? The Body of Christ is begging for a cup of the water of justice. Is it just that the voice of the status quo shouts more loudly? Do we recognize the face of Jesus when we look at people who are being treated unfairly, or does the divine spark present in each human being somehow cease to exist when the human being in question is a worker involved in a labor dispute?

"Repent!" "Change your life!" We hear these words in Scripture, spoken by Isaiah and John the Baptist (Mt 3:1–3). But what about the Scriptures we are writing today? What are the prophets saying on the south side of Chicago? This Sunday's readings promise as a prophet's reward nothing less than life itself. Do we receive the prophet? Or do we send her away thirsty? Who are the prophets in our world?

Unemployed People

"Anyone unwilling to work should not eat" (2 Thes 3:10). How easy it is to use these words to justify arguments against welfare programs and aid to the poor. How easy to pull these out of our "religion hat" when we hear about someone who is out of work.

But what about those people who are out of work, not because they *would* not work, but rather because their company was acquired or downsized and their job has disappeared? What about the man who turned fifty and found himself a "liability" to the company? What about the woman whose work was made unnecessary by new technology? What about someone who *would* work but cannot? For them this can surely seem like the end of the world. I know. It has happened in my family. With no warning at all the rug is pulled out from under you. It's as though the earth is quaking beneath your feet and a chasm of unemployment has opened and swallowed you up.

Perhaps there were warnings. Rumors often run rampant beforehand. Workers who once were friends become defensive, each protecting his or her own position, sometimes even betraying co-workers. There doesn't seem to be any way to protect yourself.

People caught in the cataclysm of unemployment often really *do* want to work—but there is no work for them to do. Today there are record numbers of people living on the edge. Numbers of homeless people are rising as entire families find themselves in need of shelter. Homelessness is no longer an automatic sign that one "would not work." Many who never thought it could happen to them now depend on us for food and shelter.

How do we respond? Paul says, "For you yourselves know how you ought to imitate us" (2 Thes 3:7). Do we?

Street People

There's a woman on the bridge. She sits like a spider up against the ironwork, knees pulled to her chest, a paper cup clasped in her hands. Rush hour commuters walk to and fro past her. Most do not even know she is there. Recently I have taken to pushing a food coupon into the cup, with a hurried "Good morning", as I walk by. But today is different. Today she pulls the cup away. "No!" And I am rejected.

Dear God, I thank you that I am not like this street woman. I go to Mass several times a week. I have a degree from a respected Catholic university. I work for the Church. My clothes are clean, attractive, and warm. I live in a nice house in a good neighborhood.

And I give food coupons to the woman on the bridge. Until she takes back her dignity which I, in my self-righteousness, have taken from her. Rejected by a street beggar. As I walk to my office I realize that I am angry. "How dare *she* reject *me?*" And then, bit by bit, a new awareness begins to emerge. Slowly my anger slips away.

This woman has claimed for herself what I would not give her. She has taken back what may be the only human dignity remaining to her, the right to say "No!" Perhaps, deep in her spirit, there is a memory that she is not invisible, that she is beautiful and beloved of God. Perhaps not. Perhaps no one ever told her. Perhaps that's why, today, she chose not to remain silent.

Today, she who was humbled has been exalted; and she who was exalted has been humbled. "God, be merciful to me, a sinner!" (Lk 18:13).

"Gaudete" People

In recent years, we have seen a spate of mergers and acquisitions. These moves usually mean layoffs for hundreds, sometimes thousands of employees. All too often, in the weeks before Christmas, thousands of people find they have no jobs. One reporter, trying to put a more positive spin on the situation, commented that at least these people probably won't go out and charge gifts only to find out later that they haven't got the income to pay for them. This may be true, but it doesn't exactly sound like cause for rejoicing!

Yet right before Christmas, on the third Sunday of Advent, that's precisely what we're told to do. *Gaudete* Sunday—the word is taken from the opening words of Paul's letter to the Philippians: "*Rejoice* in the Lord always, again I say *rejoice*" (Phil 4:4). John asks, "Are you the one?" (Mt 11:2–11). John was in prison when he asked that question, his situation not much better than what many are facing today. How might Jesus' answer look in our current situation?

"The blind regain their sight." Could having to re-think one's financial situation lead to a clearer vision of what's really important?

"The lame walk." Could this be an opportunity to move out of paralyzing complacency?

"Lepers are cleansed." Have we been trapped, or have we trapped others, in stereotypes?

"The deaf hear." What have we been too busy to hear? Could loss of a job allow us to hear differently the cries of the disenfranchised?

"The dead are raised." When a job is lost it is a kind of dying. What can I do, what kind of support can I offer, to bring new life—professionally? emotionally? financially? spiritually?

"The poor have the good news proclaimed to them." How do I proclaim the Good News—in my work? in my community? in my home?

Jesus invites us to "rejoice always." We are called to be "Gaudete" people. How do we respond to the call? How can we share the gift of joy today, in this world of mergers and acquisitions?

People with No Light in Their Eyes

They say it's El Niño, or perhaps it's La Niña. Whichever it is it looks like we're in for a long, hot summer. It reminds me of something our pastor said at Mass during a particularly hot summer spell some years ago: "If you think this is hot, just imagine what hell must be like!"

"Just imagine what hell must be like." Walking through the Loop, with the temperature hovering around 95°F and humidity over the top, certainly connects with some of our more popular images of hell. We can almost see the devil, pitchfork in hand, shoveling coal into an eternal furnace amid unbearable heat (although I'm not sure about the humidity!). But look again. There's something else going on around us that is, perhaps, a bit closer to what hell must be like.

Look into the eyes of the people you pass on the street and you'll see many things. Sometimes it's excitement (a new job? a new romance? an upcoming vacation, perhaps?). Sometimes it's sadness (a death? a downsizing? or maybe the end of a relationship?). Whatever the emotion, our lives are usually reflected in our eyes. But every so often there is an unexpected encounter and what we see is a person with no light in his eyes, someone with no life at all reflected there. Worse than sadness or pain, these eyes are without hope. "…just imagine what hell must be like!"

"Master, what must I do to inherit eternal life?" (Lk 10:25). What is required if I would have light in my eyes, rather than emptiness? "My teacher, let me see again" (Mk 10:51). And Jesus responds with a story, a story about a person who "saw." Jesus responds with a story about a person who saw the pain and suffering in another human person and did not pass by. Jesus responds with a story about an unexpected encounter in an unexpected place with an unexpected outcome. Scripture tells us that the priest and the Levite "saw" the wounded man, but did they really *see* him?

The story of the Good Samaritan is the story of four people whose paths crossed as they were going about their usual business in the usual way. But it's not just their story. The story of the Good Samaritan is also our story.

As we continue on our way, whom do we encounter in the unexpected places of our lives? What do we see when we look into the eyes of the people we live and work with? "What must we do" when we pass by the wounded and the beaten? "What must we do" when we look into the eyes of our sisters and our brothers and see no light there? When we fail to recognize the body of Christ, broken and in pain; when we cross the street and pass on the other side, "what must we do?"

"Just imagine what hell must be like…"

CHAPTER 4

What *Would* Jesus Do...

Let the wind sing to me
of changes.

Let the wind sing to me
of life...

Let *not* the wind sing to me
of caterpillar
spinning chrysalis
of denim thread...
suspended in mid-air
somewhere between
baseball
and the bomb.

Let *not* the wind sing to me
of life cut short...
of shattered images
reflected in
polluted pools.

Let the wind sing instead
of life...

Of butterflies with wings
they didn't know
they had.

Let the wind sing to me
of changes…
of flight
not *from*…
but *to*!

Let the wind sing to me
of life…

It was when I was involved in youth ministry that I wrote this poem. I was working as deanery coordinator with about two dozen parishes in an area of the city where gangs were an ever-present reality. It wasn't unusual for one of the youth ministers with whom I was working to come to me with the story of a kid who had been shot by gang members.

One evening I was driving one of my youth ministers home from an evening meeting. While we were driving he told me that three of the most violent gangs in the city were located within blocks of where we were at that moment. Shootings in the area were a nightly occurrence. After I had dropped him off (and securely locked my car!) these words started taking shape in my head.

Those of us who worked with these kids wanted so desperately for them to have a "normal" life, whatever that might be. It was incredible to think that the reason so many of them seemed unconcerned about the threat of war was that they didn't expect to live much past the age of eighteen! One boy wore his shoes to bed every night because he knew that if he left them on the floor one of his brothers would steal them. At one of the parishes I visited regularly the boys would make it a point to come out to my car with me when I left because it wasn't safe for me to be in that part of town alone after dark—and my car was parked *right in front of the rectory*!

There's a saying that has become very popular among teens today, "What Would Jesus Do?" We see the initials "WWJD" on everything from bracelets to T-shirts. And it doesn't seem to be limited to teenagers. In fact, everyone from eight to eighty is showing up with "WWJD" paraphernalia. I find myself wondering what would happen if we really took the question seriously. Would the world look any different? Would the decisions we make—whether in our corporate offices or in our union halls, our laboratories or our courtrooms—be more ethical? Would our prisons be emptier? Would our churches be fuller? Would our streets be safer? Would the wind sing again of life? If Jesus walked into our homes and our businesses, our classrooms and our factories, our boardrooms and our country clubs...what *would* Jesus do?

...If Someone Asked Him to Cheat on a Copyright Law?

"Are you a business ethicist?" Never having taken a business ethics course, I would have had to answer in the negative. Until recently, that is. Recently I heard a definition of ethics that sent me running to Webster's dictionary to check out the literal definition of the word.

Webster defines ethics as "the study of standards of conduct and moral judgment." The definition I heard at a seminar I attended recently dealing with the issues of connecting our Christian faith and our work, however, went essentially as follows: "Ethics is the societally acceptable word that means living out what it means to be a Christian in today's society." By extrapolation, then, business ethics would seem (for the Christian) to be the living out of what it means to be a Christian in the business world. Let me give you an example that came up at the seminar.

It was such a little thing, and it didn't happen very often. Use the company VCR to copy some exercise tapes—copyrighted materials (Ex 20:15). Everybody does it. "She's a single mom; she can't afford to go out and buy all of those tapes." The young woman who brought the example to our small discussion group at the conference apologized for bringing such an insignificant issue to our table. She was head of the training department of a multi-million dollar corporation. It was her responsibility to secure the VCR, as well as other multimedia equipment. The woman using the VCR was a secretary. Unfortunately, she was this woman's boss' secretary. And it was her boss who was requesting the favor.

Are you a business ethicist? How significant do the questions have to be to qualify as issues of business ethics? As Christians in the workplace, what are our standards? How do we determine what it means to be a Christian in the business world?

...If Someone at Work Asked Him for Help?

I was with a friend the other night. Laid off from her management-level job a few months ago, she is now back to work in a related industry. She talked about having seen a friend of hers, one of the managers at her previous job. He was now finding himself in the same position she had been in. A few days earlier he, too, had been laid off. "I'm glad it happened to me first," she said. "At least now I can be there for him and for his wife to help them with all of the emotional ups and downs I know they'll be going through and to just kind of tell them what to expect."

Our conversation went on to other things. To my surprise, she shared her sense that she doesn't really feel she's much of a Christian. She doesn't have "mystical" experiences, her prayer is often routine and dry, and going to Mass has become something she does out of obligation. She has trouble seeing God in her life, much less in her work.

"There was a man going down from Jerusalem to Jericho who fell prey to robbers..." (Lk 10:30–37). The priest and the Levite, both just going about their business. This "man going down from Jerusalem to Jericho" must have been something of a nuisance, an interruption in their day. But the Samaritan didn't see him that way.

Who is my neighbor? Can I see him in the new guy in the office, requesting help with a project, interrupting my day? Can I recognize her in the new secretary calling me every few minutes, asking me for information no one else will take the time to give her?

It's a funny thing: when the lawyer asked Jesus what he must do to inherit everlasting life, Jesus never said anything about going to church...

...If Someone Tried to Engage Him in Competition?

"Teacher, we saw someone driving out demons in your name and we tried to prevent him..." (Mk 9:38–40). Even two thousand years ago it would seem that the disciples were trying to establish copyright law. In their misguided efforts to maintain position and control they give us a good example of the mentality of scarcity so familiar to us in society today. While the words might not have meant anything to them, the concept of "intellectual property" would have made perfect sense.

My husband had an aunt who would gladly give out her favorite recipes but would intentionally leave out one of the ingredients! We laugh about it, but is that really so different from the employee who, in an effort to make herself look good, takes all of her files with her when she leaves her job so that her replacement will have to start every project at square one? Or the salesman who downloads the names of all his customers from the database? And what about an employee who conveniently "forgets" to tell a fellow employee when a position opens up, fearing that her more-qualified colleague might get ahead in the company before she does?

One of my favorite movies has always been *Miracle on 34th Street*. In that movie one of the employees of a major New York department store (Kris Kringle, by name) refers customers to a competitor when the merchandise they want isn't available at his store. The store psychiatrist declares him to be crazy!

During any election year the media is filled with accusations. Mysterious e-mails, personal financial records, taped phone conversations, and fuzzy photographs somehow make their way to the evening news. And we wonder why college students pass wrong answers on to fellow students to assure that they get the top grade.

God doesn't grade on a curve! God wants *everyone* to enjoy rich fare. At the abundant table of God there is no scarcity. "Would that all the people of the Lord were prophets"—and perhaps a little bit "crazy," as well...

...If He Was a Geneticist?

There's no denying that the Human Genome Project is exciting. It is being compared to the work of Darwin or Mendel. We are finding out that each individual carries in his or her DNA the entire record of evolutionary history. Mutations and re-combinations of the stuff of creation come together to make our genomes what they are today.

However, as with any discovery of this magnitude, there are dangers. One such danger is the rise of a public perception in the mass media of something called "neurogenetic determinism." "Neurogenetic determinism" equates genetic makeup with human behavior, e.g., positing the belief that a man is violent because he has a "violent gene" or that a woman is depressed because she has a "depression gene." In an article in *Commonweal* magazine Professor Stephen Rose, a British neuroscientist and geneticist, suggests that this "tendency to seek determined causes, and reductionist remedies, for our behavior generates a fatalism among those it stigmatizes. The fault, after all, lies in our genes, and moral agency is increasingly obscured and denied."

"Whoever comes to me and does not hate father and mother, wife and children, brothers and sisters, yes, and even life itself, cannot be my disciple" (Lk 14:26). Luke does not, it seems, mince words. Nor does Jesus. We are, each one of us, responsible for our choices. As we enter this genomic era of human biology we step onto holy ground. We must, therefore, remember to take off our shoes. The suggestion that we are simply a set of predetermined genetic choices denies the existence of the Holy in the sacred center of each individual. The human genome is not an "accident of nature"; it is a gift given to be owned and cherished. When we deny the gift or, worse, use it as an excuse for behavior contrary to our call to discipleship, we deny our very humanity.

Again quoting *Commonweal*, "We have the power to alter what is given as never before." We are being given new keys with which to unlock mysteries unknown to our fathers and mothers. How we choose to use them, however, remains very much in our own hands.

...If Someone Asked Him
What It Means to Be a Christian?

A woman stopped by my office the other day to ask, "How can I be more Christian in my workplace?" In other words, what should she be *saying* or *doing*? It's not an unusual question. Like so many of us, she had grown up with the idea that unless she is specifically preaching the Scriptures (with words) she isn't really being Christian. But is that really what it means to be a follower of Christ? What *does* it mean to be Christian?

A few years back, we had a young woman staying with us whose home was in Hamburg, Germany. She was hoping to find a position as an architect in Chicago, since she had spent some time there as an intern. During a conversation over dinner one evening she happened to mention that her sister was dating a young man named Christian. I commented that one of my students at the seminary was named Christian and that I thought that was an especially appropriate name for a future priest. "Oh," she said, "in Germany we don't use the word 'Christian' to designate someone who follows Jesus. We call a follower of Jesus a 'Christ.'"

The use of the word "Christ" as descriptive of one who follows Jesus gave me pause. As members of the Body of Christ, let's take a moment to ponder what this means (1 Cor 12:27). Whether it's in the workplace, the home, or wherever we find ourselves, what would it look like if we really lived what we say we believe? That is, how would our world look if we really saw ourselves not just as "Christian" but truly as "Christ" in the world?

...If He Was Asked to
Prepare a Job Description?

In his gospel, Matthew names the twelve "summoned" by Christ and tells us what they are to *do*: "cure the sick, raise the dead, cleanse the lepers, cast out demons" (Mt 10:1–8).

Throughout Scripture people are sent to do something. To the woman caught in adultery Jesus said, "Go...do not sin again" (Jn 8:11). To the rich young man, "Go...sell...give" (Mt 19:21). To Mary Magdalene, "Go...say..." (Jn 20:17). To the disciples, "Cure...raise...cleanse...cast out..." (Mt. 10:8). By virtue of our baptism we, too, are called. But too many of us act as though being "called" is enough; as though, somehow, being sent into the world ended with Christ's ascension. Being called is only the beginning of what it means to be a disciple. There is a mandate *to do* that goes with discipleship.

There is sickness in our land, in our air and in our water, in twisted bodies and confused minds—we are called to "cure the sick." There is death in our land, in war and bombing, in the eyes of the displaced and the oppressed—we are called to "raise the dead." There are lepers in our land, in the marginalized, the ill, the immigrant—we are called to "cleanse the lepers." There are demons in our land, in unemployment, substandard housing and education, addiction, oppression—we are called to "cast out demons."

At each eucharistic celebration we gather to hear the Word, break the bread and share the cup. But it mustn't end there. At the end of the celebration we are sent and we are told what we must *do*—"Go in peace, to *love* and *serve* the Lord." The world is waiting. We have been called and sent. Now, what are we *doing*?

...If Asked to Make a Choice?

"We know that all things work together for good..." (Rom 8:28). When I wrote this reflection the "search and rescue" mission for John Kennedy, Jr., his wife, Carolyn Bessette, and her sister has been changed to a "search and recovery" mission. I was deeply moved by this tragic event, as were many people around the world. The Kennedy family, which is all too familiar with tragedy, came together once more to mourn the loss of one of its own. The Bessette family mourned the loss of not one but two of its daughters. And Paul says, "All things come together for the good." What "things," we ask? What "good"?

In twelve-step circles there's a prayer. It's called the Serenity Prayer, and while it is certainly a prayer for serenity, it is also a prayer for courage and, especially, for wisdom. One thread running through all the news coverage the Kennedy plane crash, is that, of all the Kennedys, John, Jr. was the o. who most consistently made wise choices—until that Friday night when, for some inexplicable reason, he apparently chose to fly his airplane in conditions that were unsafe for someone of his skill level. It would seem from where we stand, given that we have no real knowledge of what went on that fateful evening, that it was not a wise choice.

Each one of us makes dozens of choices every day. They are not all wise choices, either. Would John Kennedy, Jr., have made a different choice if he had the chance? If we could know ahead of time how our unwise choices would turn out, would we choose otherwise?

John F. Kennedy, Jr., ran out of time to make wise choices, but we have not. We still have time to rethink the wisdom of our choices. And, if used wisely, that gift of time is one "thing" that can definitely work for the "good."

> *God grant us the serenity to accept the things we cannot change,*
> *Courage to change the things we can,*
> *And wisdom to know the difference.*

...If He Was Invited to Be on the "Tonight Show"?

A recent issue of *Business Week* magazine devoted seven pages plus its cover to "Religion in the Workplace." The story ranges all over the block, from individuals whose personal spirituality is important enough to them that they refuse to exclude it from their business life to captains of industry who, it would seem, know a profitably "good thing" when they see it. Since this is a topic in which I am most interested, I should probably be thrilled to see the increasing popularity of the subject. But I do have one concern.

My concern is that, for some, "religion" has become something of a pop commodity, the "in" thing to do. Corporate spiritual gurus are showing up everywhere, sitting in the places of honor at banquets and on evening talk shows. As a Catholic Christian whose primary focus is the marketplace I ask myself, is this really what spirituality should be about? Am I missing the mark here? Is "religion" something to be used to increase the bottom line? In other new "high priests" of marketplace religion, these "masters" ... orate soul, really who they say they are?

... Matthew reminds us that we are to have but *one* master, ... rist; that the greatest among us are to be servants to the least; and that those who exalt themselves will be humbled (Mt 23:1–12). It has happened before. Televangelists and churchmen who seem to have the world in their back pockets crash in flames while humble factory workers, without much fanfare, continue to give a fair day's work for a fair day's wages, content to live their lives with honesty and integrity.

And that's the Word we hear in Matthew's gospel—integrity, being all of-a-piece, "walking the walk." It probably won't ever make the cover of *Business Week* but I believe this is what's necessary if we're really sincere about being who—and Whose—we are called to be.

...If He Was Asked to Write Our Epitaph?

We are finite beings. We are mortal. We will die. What are we doing with our lives? Another way of posing the question might be "what would we like to see written on our tombstones?" While answers may vary, few would respond, "(S)he went to a lot of meetings!"

In Mark's version of the calling of Simon and Peter, James, and John, they immediately abandoned their nets, left their father, and followed Jesus (1:16–20). We would like to think that we would respond as quickly if Jesus came along today, but I suspect that most of us would be more like Jonah. It took being swallowed by a fish to turn Jonah around!

Following Jesus is hard work. Sometimes it seems that it would be easier to catch the next fish out of town than to drop everything and respond to God's call. But Jonah *did* respond—albeit after much kicking and screaming. Only then, after Jonah had made the decision to do what God had called him to do, did people listen and come to believe in God because of him.

This is the attractive power of God. God, in the person of Jesus Christ, draws the disciples to follow him. God, through the prophetic utterance of Jonah, draws the people of Nineveh to repent and believe (Jon 3:1–5, 10).

God, through the instruction of Paul, draws the people of Corinth to change their lives (1Cor 7:29–31).

We, too, are called to exhibit the attractive power of God in the world. How do we respond? Do we live our lives in such a way that, because of our example, others will come to believe? When our time on earth runs out and life as we know it passes away, how will we be remembered? What would we like to see written on our tombstones?

...If He Was Thinking about Getting Married?

A recent television show featured a fairy tale-like contest between several young women vying for the affection of one purportedly wealthy bachelor. The story had all the makings of a bestseller. There was a great plot, liberally laced with suspense. And there were, not one, but several beautiful princesses. Unfortunately, this particular fairy tale marriage did not have a happy ending. The groom, it appears, turned out to be the big, bad wolf!

Scripture also speaks of marriage—but not the fairy tale variety. Hosea paints a picture of a husband who pines for the lost affection of his wife (Hos 2:21–22). Mark describes a wedding feast where, in the company of the bridegroom, all the guests eat well (Mk 2:18–22). This bridegroom is very different from the tuxedo-clad millionaire on TV who, despite his supposed wealth, leaves his guests hungry and empty.

Two images. Which do we choose? Do we choose the marriage of consumerism, where "things" are valued while people are used and left hungry—or the wedding feast of human dignity, where people are celebrated and things are used? Do we choose the torn cloak, patched and faded—or the cloth newly woven and strong? Do we choose the old wine, grown weaker as the party progresses—or the wine of the new covenant, pressed from sweet grapes? Do we choose the bridegroom who yearns to have us with him for all eternity—or the bridegroom who returns from his honeymoon alone?

...If He Worked for an Advertising Agency?

People often ask, "What is God's will for me?" or, as we've been discussing here, "What would Jesus do?" These questions are asked by people genuinely concerned about finding the will of God in their lives. They seem to be looking for something "holy" or "saintly" that they can do. Expected answers might include "go to church on Sunday" or "pray the rosary" or "work in a homeless shelter."

Please don't misunderstand. These answers are not, in themselves, bad things. But if we look at Scripture we find there is another way. However, this way will require a great deal more from us. This way requires that we respond from the deepest center of our being. Paul tells the Ephesians that they must leave bitterness, fury, anger, shouting, reviling and malice behind (Eph 4:31—5:2). In other words, they must become "imitators of God." This is not only about *doing*, but also about *being*.

This way is about "compassion" and "forgiveness." If we lived this way we would, for example, treat one another very differently on our freeways. The term "going postal" would lose its currency. And physical and psychological abuse would no longer be highlighted on the evening news.

But what does bringing compassion and forgiveness into our homes, our schools, and our workplaces have to do with eating the Bread of Life? Perhaps we can get a clue from listening to some of our television commercials. Aspirin advertisements remind us that the medication we take is absorbed into our bloodstream. Nutritional supplements build up muscles and bones. What we eat has everything to do with how we feel. Jesus tells us that we must eat his flesh (Jn 6:48–51). We must allow the Son of God to be absorbed into our bloodstream, to become a part of our own body. In other words, we are called to be nothing less than the Body of Christ!

Violent behavior continues to erupt in our homes and on our streets. Newspaper headlines continue to scream the hateful ways we mistreat and abuse one another. There is a deep spiritual hunger in our society. Jesus offers himself as bread for our hunger. He offers his flesh for us to eat. How we respond, however, is up to us. Can we be life for the world? Or will we continue to be satisfied with just going to church on Sundays?

...If He Was Asked
to Run for Office?

Every day of our lives, from the time we wake up until we go back to bed at night, we make choices. "What to wear?" "What to eat?" "Say yes or say no?" Choices are a part of life.

When our daughter was thirteen and about to be confirmed she was told that she had a choice to make. Did she wish to be confirmed at this time? Most of the children in her class seemed to have no problem with the choice, but our daughter agonized over it. Did she really believe all that she had been taught? Was she ready to accept the responsibility that confirming her commitment as a Catholic Christian would require? Difficult questions. But when she finally decided to be confirmed it was a choice, not a foregone conclusion.

Most of us, at one time or another, made the choice to be confirmed. For some of us, especially those of us who were confirmed as children, it was hardly a choice at all. It was simply what one did. For others, especially those confirmed as adults, the decision most likely involved a bit more study and thought. But however we came to decide, we made a choice.

Later, as our world expanded, there were more choices to be made. "Where shall I go to college?" "Shall I marry or remain single?" "Where shall I live?" "What kind of work shall I do?" And each choice involved others. "What to study?" "Whom to marry?" "How to work?" "To whom, and for what, am I responsible?"

At the heart of it all it would seem that we are not really so very different from the disciples. Stay? or leave? (Jn 6:67). To what, to whom, do we choose to commit ourselves? Difficult questions. "Decide today whom you will serve" (Josh 24:15). In the final analysis, isn't this really the basis for *all* our choices?

...If He Was Asked to Participate in Unethical or Illegal Work Practices?

Sometimes people find themselves in situations where the person or company for whom they work is involved in unethical or even illegal practices. They'd like to leave or, at the very least, blow the whistle on the perpetrator, but they need the job. They feel vulnerable, trapped in a situation that seems to have no solution. They can't leave, but they can't stay, either. It is a time of great distress.

In the Book of Revelation one of the elders states that "the Lamb...will be their shepherd" (7:17). We've probably heard the words so often that we don't think about them, but listen again: "the Lamb...will be their shepherd." How can the lamb also be the shepherd? A lamb is small and vulnerable; shepherds are large and strong. How can the writer of Revelation place such a fragile creature in the role of caretaker? Because this lamb is not alone. This lamb is the Son of God (Jn 10:27–31).

If the lamb were alone it could easily be crushed, but even death cannot crush the Lamb of God. This Lamb knows it is held in the hand of the Father, and it is not afraid. It is usually not our situation that paralyzes us; it is our fear. The person caught in a compromising situation feels helpless and alone, paralyzed by fear, afraid to act.

It's not easy to tell someone what to do in these situations. The fact that they even ask the question, however, usually indicates that they already know the answer. But they're afraid. They feel alone and vulnerable, like a lamb among wolves. They're looking for someone to protect them, to tell them it's all right to do nothing. But it isn't. And they know it. They know they must either act to correct the situation or, in the alternative, refuse to support it; take action to change structures from within or shake the dust from their feet and move on.

It isn't an easy choice. Do we listen to the voice of the Shepherd? Or do we allow fear to have the last word? Perhaps God's answer is in the question...

...If He Came into the World Today?

John 3:16—we see the reference on billboards at sporting events and on bumper stickers. It may be truly said that the entire gospel is summarized in these verses. These words are truly cause for rejoicing. Jesus came, out of love, not to condemn but to love.

Also turning up everywhere are the letters "WWJD"—"What Would Jesus Do?" We know what Jesus did: he came into the world so that we might be saved. But sometimes it seems that we get more caught up in "condemning" than in "saving" (Jn 3:17).

We are called not only to preach the message of John 3:16 (whether on billboard or bumper sticker) but to live it. Paul tells the Corinthians, "Put things in order, listen...agree...live in peace....Greet one another with a holy kiss" (2 Cor 13:11–12). When we see John 3:16 on national television do we rejoice in our hearts that our God loves us so completely? Or are we more concerned with condemning those who do not believe as we do? God revealed Godself to Moses as merciful, slow to anger, rich in kindness. Moses bowed down in worship and invited God into his life. First Moses recognized himself in relationship with the Lord; only then did he express concern over the sinfulness of others.

"God sent his only Son into the world...not to condemn but to save." God continues to so love the world that God sends us, God's beloved daughters and sons, into our homes, our workplaces, and our communities. But what do we do when we get there? Do we encourage or put down? Do we mend our ways or tell others to mend theirs? Do we seek consensus or seek to win, no matter the cost? Do we work for peace or contribute to the chaos? The answer may be as close as the bracelet on your wrist. "What *would* Jesus do?"

CHAPTER 5

A Contradiction in Terms

Joseph and Mary left the place they knew—
to come back to the place
from which they'd first begun.

In the city of their ancestors—
there came forth a child.

In a place of unknowing—
there came forth Wisdom.

In a place of chaos—
there came forth Peace.

May this Christmas bring you
to the love of our first Father—
to the wisdom of the foolish—
to the peace for which we were created—
to the place from which
we're first begun.

A s this poem began to take shape in my head each succeeding line
seemed to contradict the one before it. Here I was, trying to come
up with a nice little greeting for our family Christmas card, but
instead of wishing "peace on earth and good will to all" I found myself
writing about tension and concepts in apparent opposition to one another. Instead of the soft, reassuring words so familiar to us at this season of

peace and love what came out were hard, challenging words demanding that we let go of what we think we know and embrace the mystery—leave the familiar to return to a place that we've forgotten we ever knew. The whole thing seemed to be a contradiction in terms. What could this possibly have to do with Christmas?

Then it dawned on me. Isn't that really what Christmas is all about? Isn't that what Jesus came to show us, that if we want to be his followers we must learn to live within contradiction, to see things differently? Common sense tells us that we need to keep working to get ahead, that no one wants to work all of his or her life just to end up back where he or she started out in the first place. Common sense tells us that it's a dog-eat-dog world out there and if we don't take care of ourselves no one else will; then Jesus tells us to sell all we have and give to the poor. In a world that values power and control Jesus tells us that we must be servants to one another. Common sense insists that while chaos might be good for the economy it rarely produces peace; Jesus insists on blessing the peacemakers. Common sense calls it foolish; Jesus calls it wisdom.

That's what my poem was trying to tell me. This poem isn't about common sense. In fact, to some people this poem might not make any sense at all. In their eyes such things as children birthing ancestors and chaos birthing peace will seem foolish. To them I say "Let's hear it for the foolish!" because by the time the poem was finished I realized that what had seemed at first glance to be a contradiction in terms was really not so contradictory after all.

See/Saw

It was just a casual exchange at the train station. The morning was cold and I was standing in line waiting to purchase a cup of coffee. The young woman ahead of me ordered a cup of hot chocolate.

"I haven't seen you in awhile," came the cheerful voice of the middle-aged woman behind the counter, "haven't you been taking the train?"

"I haven't been around for the last couple of months," the young woman replied.

"You've lost some weight, haven't you?" continued the woman.

"I had a baby. That's why you didn't see me. I was on maternity leave."

"Congratulations!" the older woman exclaimed. "That's good news!"

"Thank you!" The young woman walked away smiling, recognized, known.

A simple exchange. Nothing particularly striking or "spiritual." Or was it? There is, some say, a third eye—an all-seeing eye—God's eye, if you will—that sees into the heart. A simple exchange, a business transaction, really. But one *saw*, and one was *seen*.

"Jesus, looking at him, loved him" (Mk 10:21). We all, in the course of an average day, have many such exchanges—with family, friends, employers, employees, co-workers, store clerks, and so on. We all, in the course of an average day, look at other individuals and in some way address or respond to them. The question is, do we really *see* them?

Inside/Outside

Matthew's parable of the sower contains what I like to call "water cooler wisdom" (Mt 13:24–43). Good seed produces a good crop. Or, for members of more urban populations, ethical decision-making is good business practice.

While news accounts of major corporate scandals make headlines there are other stories, not so well publicized but perhaps more representative of what goes on every day in corporate America. For example, a young architect is involved in a minor traffic accident for which he takes full financial and personal responsibility. Months later his firm is awarded a multi-million dollar project. It turns out that the major decision-maker for the client was the other person involved in the accident. He had been impressed by the young architect's honesty and integrity and, because of that encounter, acted on his confidence that the same values would be brought to the contract.

When we read the papers and watch the news it can sometimes seem that fraud and dishonesty rule the day. "Clean up the mess" ("tear out the weeds") is often our first response. But water cooler wisdom—and the words of Jesus—say "think again," look "inside" and see as God sees.

A few days ago I was having a cup of coffee in a downtown deli. In the early morning quiet of the restaurant I thought to myself: *green chair seats pulled up to white tables. Who will sit here? What burdens will be laid down...or picked up...at these tables? What stories? plans? dreams? frustrations? hurts? failures? successes? will be discussed here today? What weight will these chairs bear? What food will be eaten here? What hungers fed? What feet will walk this wooden floor? Where will they come from? Where will they go?*

Matthew's story about the sower is a story about God's action in our lives and our response to it. In the final analysis (the "harvest" of our life), what kind of crop will we return?

Give/Get

A friend of mine is a department coordinator in a large law firm. Part of her job is to make sure that when secretaries or billing clerks find themselves with more work than they can handle, some other member of the department will be available to step in and help with the overflow. Conversely, when secretaries or billing clerks find themselves with extra time on their hands they are expected to call my friend and offer to help with overflow work. Needless to say, there is usually more overflow work to be done than there is free time available to do it!

I suspect this is because we tend to think more in terms of "scarcity" than of "abundance." We're more concerned about "getting" (as in "getting someone to help me with my work") than with "giving" (as in "using my free time to help you get your work out"). In fact, on those rare occasions when someone actually goes out of his or her way to give up what may be well-deserved break time it is so unusual that we're likely to say, "It's a miracle!"

Isaiah's invitation to "everyone who thirsts" (Isa 55:1–3) and Matthew's story of the feeding of the five thousand men plus women and children (Mt 14:13–21) are about miracles, about an understanding of life built on "abundance" rather than "scarcity." They are about feeding and being fed; about a God who offers his very body in service to us; a God who offers the sweet wine of his blood, the milk and honey of compassion. This bread we cannot buy. This wine is without cost.

Matthew's story is about Eucharist as it is celebrated in our offices and factories, our hospitals and outlet malls. Jesus doesn't provide the bread for this meal. Instead, he instructs the disciples to feed the people themselves. The bread of service cannot be purchased—it must be given. It can be very rare in the world we live in, but when we see it we know it. It brings a smile to a tired face and replaces angry words with expressions of surprise and gratitude. This celebration of Eucharist transforms the workplace—and the world—so powerfully that when we experience it we, too, are likely to say, "It's a miracle!"

Old/Young

In one of his gospel stories, Luke talks about seating arrangements at a dinner party and who deserves the best places at the table (14:1, 7–14). I was reminded of this story one day last week when I went for a walk at lunchtime, book, pen, and paper in hand. I was looking for a quiet spot away from the office, so I picked up some soup at a local carry-out store and wandered down to the river to find a table in the shade. I opened the book, took out pen and paper and began to take soup and bread out of the small brown deli sack and put them on the picnic table. That's when they arrived.

"Hello." "Hi." "My name is…" "I'm…." Two little girls appeared out of nowhere and perched like sparrows on the table. "What's that?" they asked. "My lunch," I replied. "Can we have a piece of the bread?" Three pieces of bread, three of us. It was simple math. Not only, it seemed, would I be sharing my space, but also my lunch. When a third child joined us one of the girls said "I'll break my bread in half," and without a moment's hesitation she tore off a piece to share with her friend.

They told me how old they were, and that they would soon start school. The oldest, who will be in second grade, had a book, but it had no pages. She proudly showed off her new school shoes—black plastic boots made to look like leather, with zippers on the sides. The other two, sisters, will be in kindergarten and first grade. The older one got a whole new outfit. The little one only got a new shirt, but she was happy, since she would have lots of hand-me-downs from the other two. They chattered on about their mother and her boyfriend, and about the nail in the wall by the refrigerator where one had cut her hand.

Three little girls and a grown-up lady sitting in the park. The lady works for the Church. But it was the child who broke the bread.

Challenge/Opportunity

We are becoming a very cynical society. The present generation is the first in history to have been disappointed by almost every one of society's traditionally solid institutions. Marriages are no longer made in heaven, and they don't give out gold watches at retirement parties any more. Health and education are chaotic, and air, rail, and auto transportation aren't much better. Heroes are few, and even Church and state leaders, it seems, have feet of clay. In short, there's very little in which we can put our faith these days. Yet Jesus tells us we must be prepared, ready for anything (Lk 12:35–48). But how can we be ready for anything if everything keeps changing? Well, maybe we first need to define "everything."

In 1929 the stock market crashed. People jumped out of windows. They felt they had lost everything. A man loses a job. A woman walks away from her marriage. A parent is diagnosed with Alzheimer's disease. A major employer closes its doors. These are life-changing events for which we cannot prepare. Many people are destroyed by these experiences. But others actually seem to become stronger. Why? What's the difference?

Perhaps the difference is faith. If we put our faith in human institutions (our "everything"), and those institutions break down, we have nothing left. If we put our faith in God, however, trusting God to give us "everything" that we need when things go wrong, then our faith becomes that "realization of what is hoped for and evidence of things not seen" of which Paul speaks (Heb 11:1), and life's challenges become opportunities.

Then, if human institutions fail, instead of running away from the situation we ask how we can improve it. Then, if the bond of matrimony is weakened, we ask how we might strengthen it. Believing that God always gives us what we need, when a major employer closes its doors we look for ways to care for the needs of those left without work.

God's goodness is all around us. We have been entrusted with much. But having been entrusted with much we must also take responsibility for how we use it. Do we utilize our gifts and talents to the best of our ability?

We have been entrusted with the abilities and skills necessary to nurture and support social and economic structures, but each opportunity to do good brings with it its own set of challenges. Are we willing to accept those challenges?

We are becoming a cynical society. That's the challenge—and the opportunity.

Action/Contemplation

The Scriptures are full of stories of working people. Take, for example, the stories of Abraham and Martha.

Luke's story is a familiar one (Lk 10:38–42). Martha works, "anxious about many things," while her sister, Mary, sits at Jesus' feet. This story is often used to point to prayer and contemplation as "the better part." But is that really what it's about? Is it possible that it's really about balance—and priorities?

Several years ago I was attending a parish meeting. It was a Friday evening. One member of our committee arrived late and out of breath, having driven directly from the airport. Despite the fact that it was his wife's birthday and this would be their only chance to celebrate, he had chosen to come to the meeting rather than going home to his wife. Our pastor was delighted. The rest of us, however, asked him what in the world he was doing there and told him he should go home! Balance—and priorities.

A young attorney I once worked with made it a practice to come into the office every morning at 5:00 AM, since his wife and children were still asleep and wouldn't miss him at that hour. This way he could leave at 5:00 PM and have dinner and some quality time with his family. Balance—and priorities.

Abraham's offer of hospitality to the Lord was made possible through the work he and Sarah did to prepare and serve a meal for their visitors (Gen 18:1–10A). Martha and Mary welcomed Jesus into their home. They also worked to prepare and serve a meal for him. What was different?

Perhaps it was that, while Abraham worked, he also spent quality time with his guests. For Martha, her first priority was her work, rather than the person for whom she was doing it. Balance—and priorities.

Society applauds the workaholic, that man or woman who makes lengthy "to-do" lists and then works diligently to check things off. This gospel reminds us that, while most of us are pretty good at the "work" part, it must be balanced by a genuine concern for human needs. This might be a good day to take a look at your desk calendar. Abraham? or Martha?

Top/Bottom

We've all heard the expression "Fame is fleeting." How many of us can remember which movie won the Academy Award five years ago, or which team won the World Series? Who were the Nobel Peace Prize winners? For that matter, how many of us could name our last five vice-presidents?

I must admit that I would have failed horribly on this test. And I wonder how the people who won these honors or served in these positions must feel, knowing that this is true for many if not most of us. I suspect their response would depend on how they feel about themselves and how much they identify with their achievement.

Recently I heard Fr. Richard Sparks, a Paulist priest and professor of moral theology, speak at a conference in Green Bay, Wisconsin. He explained the development of Catholic thought around moral issues and shared his belief that, in striving to lead moral lives, we all need heroes. Two of his personal heroes are President Jimmy Carter and the late Cardinal Joseph Bernardin. These two men managed to maintain their moral integrity in spite of charges of impropriety and ineptitude. They knew who they were and they lived from their centers.

Each year on Palm Sunday, we hear the story of the cries of "Hosanna" that rang out when Jesus entered Jerusalem (Lk 19:28–40). But in a few days they were replaced by shouts of "Crucify him." Even for Jesus, it seems, fame was fleeting. We may never know, this side of the kingdom, how much or how little Jesus knew about what was to come, but we do know that he lived from his center. Jesus wasn't swayed by what the crowd shouted at or about him. He knew who he was and he lived out of that knowledge.

Jimmy Carter and Joseph Bernardin are remembered for having been men of integrity. Not that they didn't care what people said about them, but at their centers they knew who they were. Can we say as much? Or are our actions governed by public opinion? Are we as willing to walk behind the donkey as we are to ride on its back?

Smart/Foolish

It wasn't too long ago (or at least so it seems to those of us who remember such things) that a single computer took up as much space as a railroad car. Today we have computers so small that tiny stylus-like instruments are necessary to work with them. All of this has precipitated what some call a "knowledge" explosion. It is quite possible that at this moment in history the information that is available to any one individual is virtually unlimited— and growing! The widespread use of computers in schools has produced a generation of children who are as comfortable with computers as people of my generation were with crayons.

But what about wisdom? Does all this information make one wise? Is knowledge the same as wisdom? The Scriptures would seem to say that Wisdom, rather than being something one learns or something to be acquired, is a gift (Wis 6:12–16). We don't have to study to acquire Wisdom, although we do have to learn to recognize it when we see it.

The wise virgins had wisdom; the foolish did not (Mt 25:1–13). Here we have another clue. We all know people who, while very smart, can also be very foolish. In fact, most of us have, on occasion, acted foolishly.

The Book of Wisdom speaks of the perfection of prudence. The wise virgins were prudent; they planned ahead. But this is more than keeping your DayTimer updated. This is about "gift." And what's more, this gift is ours to keep, for "Wisdom is radiant and unfading...." That means it will never crash or need to be reprogrammed!

So let us prepare for the future, not with the prudence of those who hide their money in the mattress but with the prudence born of Wisdom. And since this Wisdom is available to everyone it doesn't matter if you can operate a computer or not. The gift of Wisdom is waiting for "those who love her and seek her," and that's all of us, even if some of us *are* old enough to remember a time when there were no computers!

Education/Wisdom

In a perfect world I would be a perpetual student. I started taking college courses when my children were in junior high and completed my master's degree in my forties. I read voraciously, devour workshops, and attend college classes whenever and wherever available. I like to think of myself as being well educated. But the Scriptures don't talk about education, they talk about *wisdom* (Wis 7:7–11), and that makes all the difference.

It was about four years ago. The woman in my office had stopped by before going to her waitress job in a nearby restaurant and after finishing her work of cleaning the priests' residence in our parish complex. She came with a question about prayer.

The single mother of three active teenagers, when she was not working she could often be found on the playground umpiring a softball game, helping out as a crossing guard after school, or making deliveries in her secondhand station wagon for the parish St. Vincent De Paul Society. She seldom had the luxury of quiet time for prayer and had become very good at finding God in the noise and confusion of her life. But she was concerned. Sometimes when she was busy with some mindless task, like cleaning bathrooms, she would find herself reflecting on her relationship with God and wondering what God's will for her might be. She would get into conversations with God, asking what she must do, and in these moments of solitude God would speak to her. Knowing that I gave workshops on prayer she had come to ask me if this was all right.

This young woman had barely completed high school. She did not have an advanced degree in theology. But in her simple and direct approach to God she taught me about wisdom. I knew *about* prayer; she *knew* prayer. I spoke *about* God; she spoke *to* God. I looked for the word of God in books; she encountered the Word of God in all the reflections and thoughts of her life.

I assured the young woman that her way of prayer was surely pleasing to God. Then I went home to clean my bathroom.

Feast/Famine

"Artificial intelligence"—an expression used to describe computerized calculations and tasks similar to human thinking but generally beyond the capability of the human brain. Unfortunately, we've come to believe that computers are smarter than humans. And so it may be, if this is how we measure "intelligence."

When Jesus refers to himself as "living bread" and invites the people to eat his flesh and drink his blood the people question what he could mean by these words (Jn 6:51–58). Taken literally, what Jesus is describing borders on cannibalism! In fact, that's probably how a computer would interpret his invitation. Let's take another example. What would a computer make of the statement that a person "will live forever"? Being very literal, the computer would likely assert that it's impossible for the human body as we know it to live forever.

But we are not computers, and this is not computer language. This is sacramental language. One might compare it to poetry or music. The meaning is the same, but we must listen differently if we are to understand. The writer of Proverbs reminds us that there is a difference between intelligence ("artificial" or otherwise) and wisdom (Prov 9:1–6). Wisdom sets an abundant feast and invites everyone to eat and drink. No one goes away hungry or thirsty. Intelligence, on the other hand, confines its guest list to quantifiable data and facts. It is a system defined by limitation. It leaves unsatisfied those who come hungry to its table.

The questions generated by our fast-paced society and ever-expanding social, political and economic systems demand faster, more complex answers. We have become programmed, like so many computers, to depend on the verifiable and provable. We have sworn allegiance to intelligence. And it has left us hungry. Potential employers look at an applicant's IQ, but no one has ever devised a "WQ" (Wisdom Quotient) test. What is verifiable and provable is what counts, no matter that it cannot satisfy our deeper hunger.

Jesus invites us to feed on his body, to drink his blood. Do we accept Wisdom's invitation? Or do we settle for the sparse offerings of "artificial intelligence"?

Darkness/Light

In Mark's gospel Jesus describes things beyond the imagination of the people to whom he is speaking (13:24–32). "The sun will be darkened...the moon will not give its light...the stars will be falling from the sky...the powers in the heavens will be shaken." Surely such things could never happen! But they do happen. Today we understand what causes an eclipse of the sun or of the moon, and TV meteorologists predict meteor showers almost to the minute. Today there is little we cannot imagine.

Or is there? Who could ever have imagined the results (or lack thereof, depending on your perspective) of our national elections in the fall of 2000? With no clear winner in the presidential elections in what is arguably the most powerful nation on earth it seemed that, indeed, "the powers in the heavens" were shaken. But it wasn't the end of the world. Rather, for those responsible for the electoral process, the lessons learned from that experience resulted in the development of less confusing and more effective methods of casting our ballots.

But there are other things, difficult things, things too painful to imagine. There are wars and rumors of wars. There are diseases capable of wiping out entire populations. And in the richest country in the world there are children who go to bed hungry. The signs of the times, it seems, are often written in blood. And while political promises may disappear like so many damaged ballots, our responsibility as citizens of our country and of our world does not disappear.

Wise men and wise women still speak. The Word of God has not passed away. But we must listen if we are to hear, for the machinery of politics can make a mighty noise. Great things are possible if we would only dare to imagine them. The world has not come to an end. God has given us another day. How will we use it! Will we be light for the world shining "brightly like the splendor of the firmament" (Dan 12:1–3). Or will we be content to sit idly in front of our television sets, watching the evening news and placidly cursing the darkness?

CHAPTER 6

Swimming Against the Tide...

A square more holes than linen
for his hanky;
A bristly, smiling, hobo clown
named "Frankie."

A sad, tramp, hobo clown
with happy face;
He wears his rag-tag suit
with charm and grace.

A cardboard box from K-Mart
for his bed—
A tattered felt fedora
on his head—
He doesn't share from pockets
lined with gold;
He shares his coat
when someone else is cold.

He doesn't give a
dinner party for eight;
His love is food for
those half-starved with hate.

In worldly terms he doesn't
own a thing;

But still he smiles—
a jester for the King.
He's neither short nor very tall.
He's neither stout nor lanky.
He's just the right size for a hug.
He's a hobo clown
named "Frankie."

Let me set the scene. It's a cold Monday morning in early October, October 4 to be exact. Like so many people I've talked to lately I'm nursing a cold, so I just ran across the street to McDonald's to get a large glass of orange juice. Outside, people are walking around with their hands shoved in their pockets, jackets pulled up around their ears. It's hard, at this time of year, to know what to wear.

The people in Matthew's gospel seem to be having the same problem. The gospel is about a wedding feast, and wearing the right clothes. What is the appropriate attire for the wedding feast?

In the first reading Isaiah describes rich food and choice wines and a loving God who wipes every tear from one's eye. People were standing lined up at McDonald's waiting, even at this early hour, for burgers and fries. How are we fed? What intoxicates us? How do we love? Do we know how to live, as Paul says, in "humble circumstances" as easily as in "abundance"?

Today, as I write, it is the feast of St. Francis of Assisi. As a Secular Franciscan I am committed to the vision of Francis, a vision not limited to vowed religious but a vision for everyone, a vision of the kingdom lived out in the world, in homes and schools and downtown office buildings, in the finest restaurants and at McDonald's.

Many years ago I was involved in clown ministry. A friend of mine, also a Secular Franciscan and a clown minister, adopted the name "Frankie." I wrote this poem for her. It's a poem about Francis' vision of the kingdom and what proper attire for admission might be. Today, in the spirit of the Scriptures and of St. Francis, I share it with you.

...On the Job Site

I once had occasion to discuss Matthew's gospel about the landowner who went out at various times during the day to hire laborers (20:1–16A) with a group of men who have worked as day laborers and/or as union members. When I first read the story most of them agreed with the outraged workers who, in Matthew's words, "grumbled against the landowner." And I must admit that, until recently, I totally agreed with them. Taken from the point of view of the workers hired early in the day it's easy to see why this story would be a union worker's nightmare.

Let's look at it from a different point of view—that of the landowner. First of all, it's obvious that the man knows nothing about business. Not only does he not understand that the amount one is paid is traditionally determined in direct proportion to the amount of time one works; he doesn't even understand that it's up to the workers to come in and apply for the job and not for the employer to go out looking for them! Just what is Jesus trying to say? How can this landowner—who doesn't think at all like we do—even begin to show us what God is like?

Perhaps, if we are going to understand the story, we must first examine how we think. We think about things as we've always thought about them. What Jesus seems to be telling us, however, is that that's not how God thinks. We hold back; God gives everything away. What's more, God doesn't wait in some employment office in the sky for us to come in to apply for the job; God comes out looking for us!

Once I began to look at this parable from God's perspective instead of from my own I began to realize just how exciting it really is. To a worker, this kind of thinking makes absolutely no sense; but to the recipient of the generosity of this God it is the ultimate in good news! In fact, perhaps precisely because of my position as a worker, this parable has now become one of my favorites. And after explaining it to those day laborers and union workers I have a feeling that it may become one of theirs, as well.

...In the Steno Pool

"Name one ethical dilemma you have been faced with over the last few months." A workshop instruction. A secretary filling out the application for the workshop on business ethics, Sue was surprised by the question. Her immediate response was, "I'm not important enough to be asked to make ethical decisions in my work."

But, when she looked more closely at her day-to-day business activities, Sue realized that this wasn't totally true. She had to agree that, even though the decisions involving ethical considerations increase in complexity as one moves to higher levels of management, the issues exist, in one form or another, at every level. For us as Christians ethics must somehow be connected to the way we conduct ourselves in our work in light of our faith, regardless of what rung we occupy on the corporate ladder. Whether one suspects that a co-worker is "borrowing" supplies from the office or doing a little "grocery shopping" in the company cafeteria, or that an executive is making "unusual" arrangements in order to land a major contract, an individual must take an ethical stand.

"Name one ethical dilemma you have been faced with over the last few months," whether butcher, baker, candlestick-maker—or secretary... (Mt 25:14–30).

...In the Law Office

Joanne was an attorney. Growing up on a farm in Iowa, it had always been her dream to make her life in the big city. During her years at law school she had developed a reputation as a dogged researcher. Her attention to detail gave her an almost uncanny ability to read a situation and to take appropriate action. It was no surprise when, even before graduation, she was offered a coveted position in the corporate department of a large, multinational law firm.

Over the next five years Joanne worked hard. She put in long hours, often working far into the night. She married Bill, her college sweetheart, and the two of them set out in pursuit of the American dream. Anticipating early partnerships with their respective firms, Joanne and Bill determined to do whatever it took to accomplish their goal.

It was during one of their all-too-brief visits home to Iowa that everything changed. Joanne's sister and her husband were there with their two-year-old, and it was as though Joanne was seeing them for the first time. In fact, it had been six months since they had been together, even though they lived within only a few hours' drive of one another. Sitting there on the living room floor playing with the baby, Joanne began to wonder what it was that she and Bill were giving their lives to. Surely there was more to life than working twenty-four hours a day, seven days a week (Mt 16:26). Joanne began to wonder if perhaps, in her attention to detail, she was somehow missing the bigger picture.

It was not an easy decision but before the year was out Joanne gave notice at the firm. Bill had been offered a position as in-house counsel to an Iowa corporation. The road would not always be smooth. There would be difficult days ahead. Business associates secretly, and sometimes not so secretly, accused them of having lost their senses. But Joanne and Bill had crossed over the line of caring what others thought of them. For perhaps the first time in their life together they dared to believe that life was about more than salaries and stock options. And Joanne was pregnant.

...In the World of Finance

It is with no small amount of pride that I tell you that I am an exceptional credit risk. Why, last week alone I received no fewer than seven letters informing me that, due to my impeccable credit history, I have been selected to receive a credit card at the lowest interest rate available. All I have to do is say "Yes." But as good as the offer may look on paper, there's one problem. I could end up borrowing beyond my means, be unable to repay the loan, and thereby lose my stellar credit rating!

But what about lending? Obviously the credit companies who made me these offers would demand repayment. If I borrowed without repaying I could be in serious legal difficulties, and rightly so. But in Matthew's gospel

Jesus tells us to lend without expecting anything back (18:26). What does he mean by that? No business could survive that way.

Perhaps the reason Jesus' words seem to contradict everything we think we know about business is that the gospel was never intended to be used as a business operations manual. Businesses are operated to make a profit; Scripture asks, "What does it profit one to gain the whole world and lose one's immortal soul?" Is it really ethical to extend credit, knowing full well that unsuspecting persons might be plunged into a downward spiral of debilitating debt?

And then there's that matter of "love your enemies" (Lk 6:27–38). Perhaps we need to reconsider the meaning of "love." When we love only on the condition that the beloved will love us in return, could it be that we are not so much loving them as we are loving ourselves? God did not "loan" Jesus to us, expecting us to somehow repay the debt out of our own resources. Rather, God poured out love in a river of blood that continues to flow each time we gather for Eucharist. And then God said, "Do this in remembrance of me."

Every week God extends no fewer than seven invitations to us to wake up, to accept that we are loved unconditionally, to give as it is given to us, and to forgive as we have been forgiven. There's no interest due and the reward is great. The envelope is stamped and self-addressed. All we have to do is say "Yes."

...In Decision Making

Jesus' parable in Luke's gospel about the man who wishes to construct a tower (14:25–33) reminds me of a conversation my husband and I had recently with our son. For the last year or so he has been renting a small house with the understanding that he will do necessary renovation work in exchange for rent. Now it seems the owner is so pleased with his progress that she has decided to sell the house. Our son is faced with the decision of whether to buy this house or look for another place to rent. Our advice— be sure you look carefully at your financial situation before you commit yourself to starting something you might not be able to finish.

Jesus gives similar advice. He advises that the man must "calculate the outlay to see if he has enough money to complete the project." Similar advice, but much higher stakes. Jesus is talking about nothing less than the cost of discipleship. This is not about buying a house. This is about making a commitment to follow the gospel.

In Paul's letter to Philemon (9B–10, 12–17), we hear the challenge put another way. Onesimus, a slave, had run away from Philemon. This clearly opposed the social order of the day. Legally, Philemon would have been justified in demanding retribution. But Paul appeals to Philemon. Having been baptized by Paul, Onesimus is now Philemon's brother in faith. Each has chosen to commit his life to Christ. Can Philemon honor his commitment?

We face dilemmas like this every day. As Christians we are committed to living the gospel; but as workers and citizens in twenty-first century America we often face social and economic situations and choices that challenge gospel values. This is the cost of discipleship. This is what it means to commit one's life to Christ.

Like Paul in his letter to Philemon, and my husband and I in our conversation with our son, Jesus advises us to use wise judgment before making so serious a commitment. Can we remain committed to the gospel, even when it means going against the accepted social and economic conventions of our workplace? our neighborhood? perhaps even our own homes? Are we willing and able to pay the cost of discipleship?

...In Sharing Intellectual Property

Recently I was with a group of people discussing ways to bring Christian values into the workplace. Several ideas were suggested, but one struck me as particularly challenging. It had to do with the role of the "mentor."

"Mentoring" is not a new concept. It has a long and proud tradition in Church circles, where it's called "discipling." In Scripture we read about the rabbi and his students, or Jesus and his disciples. But it also has its place at work, where the individual being mentored might be called an apprentice or an intern. Whatever the designation or circumstance, mentoring occurs whenever someone who knows more about something shares knowledge and/or experience with someone who knows less.

What is new is that there has arisen a marked hesitation to offer mentoring. These days, as corporations become increasingly concerned about "intellectual property," some people have become less willing to offer to share what they know. Maybe it's because they're afraid that they will no longer be needed. Maybe they're worried that someone younger (and, consequently, willing to work for a lesser salary) will replace them. Whatever the reason, these people doggedly refuse to accept the role of mentor.

The story of Mary and Elizabeth in Luke's gospel is also about mentoring (1:39–56). But, as in so many gospel stories, there is a twist. Here it's not just the elder mentoring the younger, but also the younger mentoring the elder. Each of the women brings her own insight and experience to the encounter, and each is enriched by the other. What a wonderful example of poverty! In giving it all away, all is given. In owning nothing, one possesses it all.

But how can we translate this back into the workplace? How can we let go of fear and take a chance that in sharing our knowledge and experience we will be left richer, rather than poorer? Mary stepped out in faith. She sought a mentor in Elizabeth and brought blessing to Elizabeth in return. Is there someone we can mentor along the way to building up the kingdom? Do we have the courage it takes to be vulnerable? Are we willing to accept the challenge?

...In the Voting Booth

"My kingdom does not belong to this world...everyone who belongs to the truth listens to my voice" (Jn 18:33B–37). Where is this "kingdom" Jesus is talking about? And what is this "truth" he refers to? One can understand "listening" to the truth, but how can one "belong" to the truth?

Jesus proclaims himself to be king, but only after Pilate asks him if he is a king. Even then Jesus is quick to point out that he is not a king in the usual sense. So we are probably safe to assume that he is not speaking of "this world" in the usual sense, either.

In the political world a king represents human power and authority. It is the king who is served. But Jesus teaches that in his kingdom that one who would be served must be servant. This is the "truth" to which we belong.

Jesus, though God, chose to become human. His truth and his kingdom, then, exist not just on the spiritual level but on the physical level as well.

In baptism we were anointed into Christ as priest, prophet, and king. This is the kingship and the kingdom that we inhabit today, right now—not some future kingdom that we will one day inherit but the kingdom that was at the beginning and will continue until the end of time. But sometimes we forget. Sometimes we forget that we are called to live the truth of the kingdom in the voting booth and at the ballot box. Sometimes we forget that we are called to live the truth of the kingdom in the grocery store and behind the wheel of our car.

Pilate saw only what was visible to the eye; we must remember to see with the eyes of faith. Pilate heard only the words of jealous power; we must remember to listen to the Word made flesh. We must remember because this is the truth to which we belong. We must remember because this is the kingdom we are called to build every day—and in every circumstance—of our lives.

...In Choosing a Job

Over the past several years, in addition to working full time as a real estate agent in one of the city's more affluent suburbs, raising her children, and keeping up with all the demands of life as a busy wife and mother, Diane had been working on a master's degree in social work. She hadn't really given much thought to what she would do after she got her degree but she did know, in some vague way, that if she chose to change jobs it would probably mean a significant decrease in income.

Then one day, out of the blue, Diane got a phone call. The agency where she had done her internship was interested in hiring her. Would she like to come in for an interview? When she looked back on it later Diane would wonder what had made her say "yes" but, whatever the reason, that's precisely what she did. And a few days later she found herself giving notice to her boss at the real estate office.

Diane's boss was surprised. She tried to talk Diane out of leaving, but agreed to abide by her decision. Diane left feeling relieved but vaguely uneasy. It had been almost too easy. The next morning her suspicions were confirmed. Calling her into her office, Diane's boss started to suggest alternatives. They could rearrange her hours so that she could do *both* jobs. Besides, agencies in the suburban area were more prestigious than those in the inner city, and Diane's chances for advancement would be greater there. Her boss also hinted at a possible partnership and increased percentage bonuses.

Diane was stunned. The offer was tempting. It would result in more money, more power, and more prestige (Mt 4:1–11). But then she smiled and said, "No, thank you. I really appreciate all that you're trying to do, but I've made up my mind." Her boss had spoken in the language of economics, the only language she understood. But Diane knew that this was not about economics. And Diane had made her choice.

...In the Family

In the recent rash of anti-smoking television commercials one stands out in my mind. A young man speaks, identifying himself as the grandson of the founder of a major cigarette manufacturing company. My response to the ad is, "He must mean what he's saying, to speak out with such honesty; and I bet his family is really mad at him!" Sometimes it can be very difficult to speak the truth—and very unpopular.

Politicians depend on popularity. Some start out with good intentions but soon realize that good intentions don't guarantee votes. Running for office is expensive, and political donations can carry a hefty price tag. In circumstances like these it can be difficult to maintain your moral equilibrium. One day you wake up and find you hardly recognize the face that looks back at you in the mirror. But what are you supposed to do when to speak out could spell political suicide? It's not easy to confront those whose money finances your campaign.

As children we all want to be popular. Take the unfortunate example of the teen who, in his search for acceptance, is drawn into a gang. Realizing his mistake, he tries to leave. But standing up to a gang can be dangerous and such efforts are rarely successful. All too often we read the grim outcome in the morning paper while television cameras capture a family's pain at the loss of their child.

It takes courage to set the earth on fire. Facing evil is not an easy position to maintain. It isn't easy to walk away, whether from a gang whose displeasure can destroy your life or from a political party whose displeasure can destroy any chance you may have of being re-elected. But it's especially difficult to walk away from your family, for the displeasure of your family can destroy your heart.

Jesus knew what it meant to lose his life. Jesus knew what it meant to lose his reputation. Jesus knew what it meant to swim against the tide. But he never lost heart; never gave up. When his Father spoke he replied "not my will but thine be done" (Lk 22:42), and with those words the fire was started (Lk 12:49). The question remains—do we have the courage to tend the flame?

CHAPTER 7

Contract or Covenant?

"Cast your net out
on the other side..."

In the dark—
one side
looks much like the other.

In the dark—
a voice calls out
across the water:

"Cast it now—
your net—
out on the other side."

In the dark—
one trusts
the voice.

Two fishermen cast nets
out
in the dark.

One knows the lake...
the Other
knows the fish.

This is a poem about change. It's about leaving the familiar behind and setting out in a new direction. It's about embracing change, even when it brings pain.

Sometimes we choose change. Sometimes it's some new challenge—maybe a new job, or a new home. This kind of change can be exciting, even exhilarating. Sometimes change comes, not because we choose it, but because we have made a commitment to something or someone and change is necessary if we are to honor our commitment. This kind of change can be difficult. This poem is about this second kind of change.

The man had been our pastor for several years. He was our priest, and he had become our friend. And now he was being transferred. I wrote the poem as a "good-bye" present. No one wanted him to leave, but he had made a commitment to God. Now God was calling him to honor that commitment. It was time to make a change.

The Sunday after he gave us the news I heard this gospel passage and it seemed that God was speaking directly to my heart. This was to be my gift to our pastor. I was to give him permission to go, to let him know that we understood that his covenant with God was stronger than his contract with the parish, and to share my conviction that God had even bigger and better things in store for him in the future.

Two relationships—one, our priest's relationship with us; the other, his relationship with God. As human beings we tend to think in terms of human relationships, but God does not think as we do. Human beings enter into contracts; God enters into covenant. Contracts come to an end; God's covenant is everlasting. And while human beings may choose to break covenant with God, God never breaks covenant with us.

Our priest would not have to make the change alone. We knew—and he knew—that God would be there with him in the boat when he responded to God's voice and cast his net on the other side.

Eucharist

"He just eats it up." We've all heard the expression. Often it's praise, heaped on an individual, that is being referred to. Sometimes we hear it in the workplace referring to someone's passion for a challenge, some new problem to be solved, or the task of finding new ways to save time and money. Sometimes it's increased responsibility that the individual thrives on. Sometimes it's the power that goes with that responsibility. "He just eats it up."

Compare that with another expression: "You are what you eat." Nutritionists like to use this one when touting the value of a balanced diet. In a Christian context it reminds us of what we profess during the ritual celebration we call the Eucharist. Not only are we identified with what we eat, but it becomes the very stuff of which we are made, "the blood of the covenant" (Mt 26:28).

Two common expressions we hear every day. Heard in a Christian context, they pose serious questions for our lives. Where is our passion? Do we really believe that we are what we eat?

The Golden Rule

The question was asked recently (with regard to business), "Is the Golden Rule too naive?" Do we do unto others as we would have them do unto us? Or are we more concerned about doing unto others *before* they do unto us?

We probably need to start by asking what, exactly, we would have them do? Do we expect honesty in our working world? Do we share information and trust others to share information with us? What about those people we thought were our friends but who, we find, are willing to use information about any misstep of ours to further their own agenda, regardless of the pain it may cause for us or for the organization? How do we respond to them? What do we do about the "users," people who see only the satisfaction of their own needs and couldn't care less about the needs and well-being of their colleagues?

Is it realistic to expect to find virtues like fairness, self-discipline, and personal accountability in the corporate setting? Jesus calls us to love as He loves, unconditionally. But how does the principle of unconditional love translate to the workplace? (*Does* the principle of unconditional love translate to the workplace?) Is a "covenant violation" really any different from a "contract violation"?

In Matthew's gospel Jesus tells us to "fear no one" (Mt 10:26–33). The message would seem to be that there is more to life than being successful—if success must be bought with secrets spoken in the dark. But we still have to put food on the table, pay the mortgage, secure healthcare benefits, and plan for retirement. Sure, the Golden Rule sounds good on paper, but a person's got to do what a person's got to do, right? It's a dog-eat-dog world out there and sometimes, instead of honesty, it's those whisperings in the dark that rule the day.

These are hard questions. Do we "do unto" or are we "done unto"? Whom can we trust? What are the rules? *Is* the Golden Rule too naive?

Relationship

In John's gospel we hear a story about things that get in the way. Money changers, for a fee, exchange Greek and Roman coins for the Temple currency necessary to purchase animals to be offered as sacrifice so that one might be put in right relationship with God. Jesus' actions say that being in right relationship with God is not something to be bought and sold. His own body will be the acceptable sacrifice. People and their laws have gotten in the way.

We tend to think of the Ten Commandments as "laws" that we must keep if we don't want to get into trouble. But God gave the commandments so that all might be well with the people with whom God had chosen to enter into covenant. God gave the commandments as opportunities for the people to enter into, and remain in, right relationship with God with one another.

The commandments remind us of all the wonderful things God has done for us. Why would a people ever want any other god besides this One? But the people do take other gods. In fact, in some ways the commandments themselves become their god, and they get in the way.

The people look for signs and wonders. But they want the signs and wonders for themselves rather than as guides pointing to God, and the signs and wonders become the gods. They get in the way.

This Scripture passage reminds us that outer actions can get in the way of an inner reality. The animals in the temple are set free. The way to God cannot be bought and sold; it is the possession of no one and of everyone. The way to God is Jesus. We confuse the message with the messenger until the messenger becomes the god. We confuse the way with the means until the means becomes the god. We confuse being in relationship with God with keeping the rules until the rules become the god. We confuse having our own way with the Way, and in the process our own way becomes the god.

What is the reality of our relationship with God? Is God truly at the center of our lives? Or are there things in our lives that are getting in the way?

Employment

The topic under discussion was loyalty in the workplace. Does it still exist? People who remember a time when people worked one job all their lives and then retired with a gold watch mourn the loss of those days. Others believe that workplace loyalty hasn't disappeared, only changed. For many, given the rapidly changing nature of the workplace, loyalty to employers, employees, and co-workers may actually have become more, rather than less, important.

What does loyalty in the "new" workplace look like? One man describes it as standing up for others. When gossip starts, put an end to it. When someone's reputation is being torn down, build it up. Instead of saying something for which you might later be sorry, walk away. For him, being loyal to one's co-workers means, at the very least, that we don't participate in tearing them down.

The problem is, people don't always like it when we respond this way. "Everybody does it," they say, in defense of their actions. Or, "It's always been this way; the only way up the ladder is to shove the other guy out of the way." But Jesus tells us to love one another, and love presupposes loyalty. If we are truly to love one another, then it follows that we must be loyal to one another, and ripping apart someone's reputation is simply out of the question. Why don't people like it when we refuse to go along with them? Maybe it's because by refusing to participate we are, in effect, holding a mirror up to their actions and they don't like what they see reflected there.

For many of us, this can be a new way of thinking. "Behold, I make all things new" (Rev 21:1–5A). In John's gospel we read, "I give you a new commandment: love one another" (13:34). Love and loyalty go together. It was said of the early Christians, "See how they love one another." If someone were to listen in on the conversations around the coffee machine in your office, what would they say about *you*?

Humanitarianism

They are sixty-three of the best and the brightest. Young men and women representing all four years at the university, these young people will one day make decisions that will affect the future of the world.

The theme of the retreat was vocation. As the weekend progressed several voiced their concern that perhaps they should transfer from global finance to something in the not-for-profit area. The speaker quickly assured them that their expertise will be needed precisely where they are heading, that is, out in the world. One day they will sit in corporate boardrooms and direct the course of business around the globe. They will make decisions that will impact the lives of thousands, if not millions, of people. Theirs will be the incredible, but often thankless, task of building up the kingdom.

Lately there has been a great deal of conversation about the fact that our country has helped other nations by providing healthcare, food, and technical assistance. These discussions often conclude with the words, "and what thanks do we get?" In Luke's gospel we find a story about giving thanks (17:11–19). Ten lepers stand at a distance from Jesus. They do not call "unclean" but, rather, "Jesus, Master, have pity on us!" Obviously they have heard of this man, Jesus. They believe he has the power to heal them, to determine whether they will live or die. Luke tells us that all ten were cleansed but that only one (and that one a despised foreigner!) returned to say "Thank you."

They were cleansed "as they were going." Perhaps the other nine simply continued to do as Jesus had instructed them and would return later, after showing themselves to the priests. Perhaps the Samaritan, not being a Jew, didn't feel obliged to obey this particular law. Whatever the case,

Jesus didn't somehow "repossess" the cleansing of the nine because they neglected to thank him. God's love is unconditional; it doesn't depend on anything we do—or don't do.

Those university students may one day find themselves faced with decisions that could determine whether foreign populations will live or die. Let us hope that they, like Jesus, might find it in their hearts to act without demanding a "Thank you."

Parenthood

Maria was a single mother, working hard to put her two children through school. The oldest child of immigrant parents, she knew how difficult life could be. She encouraged her children to think about the future (Heb 12:5-7, 11-13). She wanted so much for them to be able to go on to college. But Maria's children made other choices.

Instead of preparing for college they played their way through high school, cutting classes and refusing to study for those they did attend. Her son barely managed to graduate. Finally, realizing that his future would consist of low paying jobs in fast food restaurants, he decided to enlist. In the Army he chose to continue his education. It wasn't easy but eventually he managed to get his college degree. Now he finds new doors are opening for him and he's trying to decide whether he will reenlist when his time is up or pursue a career outside the military.

Unfortunately, Maria's daughter made other choices. She chose to drop out of high school before graduation. When she worked it was at low paying jobs and she soon gave up, choosing instead to borrow money from Maria or, when she refused, from her friends. Eventually Maria had to ask her to leave, and the girl moved in with her boyfriend. She got pregnant. Her baby is two years old now, her boyfriend long gone. She's living on public assistance, working on and off as a waitress but mostly staying home. Maria still loves her daughter. She worries about the baby. And she cries a lot.

God gives us choices. God gives us everything we need. It is our choice whether to accept or reject God's gifts. God loves us as we are, unconditionally. It is our choice whether or not we will love God in return. God prepares a place for us in God's kingdom. It is our choice whether or not to enter. God has given us the gift of free will. How we choose to use it, however, is entirely up to us.

Society

This year I somehow found myself spending the Fourth of July alone in a crowd of several hundred people. Knowing that I would have some time to kill before dark I had brought a book with me, *The Threefold Way of Saint Francis* by Murray Bodo, OFM. Bodo told how, as he was preparing to leave the office of the famous Dr. Karl Menninger to fly home to New Mexico, he told Menninger that he dreaded changing planes at Chicago's O'Hare Airport. Menninger asked him to try something. "When you change planes at O'Hare Airport you'll probably have a serious walk to your connection. Instead of setting your teeth and walking determinedly to your plane, try to make eye contact with as many people as you can, loving them with your eyes."

It sounded like good advice, something I'd have to try on my next trip through O'Hare. Then I looked up. Engrossed in my book I hadn't realized that people were arriving in droves, and some of them were claiming territory practically on top of mine! Children were lighting sparklers. A man with a puppy walked right over my feet. Thoughts of "How dare they!" and "They'd better not stand up during the show!" flashed through my brain.

"You shall love the Lord, your God, with all your heart...and your neighbor as yourself" (Lk 10:25–37). Love isn't up in the sky, like some kind of heavenly fireworks display. Wednesday night my neighbor was sitting right next to me, puffing on a Camel. And somehow I knew that Dr. Menninger was talking to me. Not sure what to expect, I began making eye contact with people, "loving them with my eyes." And, can you believe it? They smiled back! I didn't have to go across the sea at all; love was right there in the park.

"Who is my neighbor?" The man with the puppy; the child with the sparklers—each carries the divine spark within them. Love is all around us, but sometimes it's hard for us to see. Why do we find this so difficult to understand? Well, maybe it's because we haven't yet learned to look with our hearts.

The Organization

"Love," "truth," and "delight"—the words jump out at us from Paul's Letter to the Romans (5:1–5) and from Proverbs (8:22–31). Let's try a little experiment. Imagine, if you will, a flow chart showing corporate officers and their areas of responsibility, a kind of "God chart." At the top, right in the middle, is "God"; beneath it are "Father," "Son," and "Spirit"; and on the next line are the words "love," "truth," and "delight." Of course, the doctrine of the Trinity took centuries to develop, and we cannot even begin to capture it here, but let's continue and see where our "God chart" image takes us.

Under the word "Father" we find "love." This might surprise some people. They picture God as a kind of master accountant with a divine spreadsheet keeping track of our sins. But for those of us who have come to know God as a God of love, rather than of judgment, there's no surprise here. Next is "truth." Again, no surprise; we recognize Jesus as the Word, the Truth of God. But the last box is different. "Delight!" This is a God who finds "delight in the human race." This is very different from a God who finds fault in the human race, or from a God who finds duplicity in the human race. Can we even begin to take it in? Our God finds delight in us!

And then the flow chart gets all mixed up. The boxes in the top rows merge, and the words in the third row rearrange themselves. "Truth" and "love" flow out through Spirit, and the Son takes such delight in our humanness that the Word becomes flesh. Finally, merged in love, dancing with delight, on the next line the truth of our God flows out into our lives—one box, connected to all those above it, labeled "you and me." All of the love and truth and delight of God flow into and through that box.

What happens next? Well, that's pretty much up to us, because at this point the "God chart" begins to add new lines and get all mixed up with the rest of our lives. Where do we find God's "delight," "love," and "truth"? How do we conclude the experiment? How are we filling in the blanks?

The Family

Once upon a time there were two brothers and a sister. Each of the brothers had a wife; the sister, a husband. One day, realizing that their widowed mother was no longer able to live alone, it was decided that one of the brothers and his family would move into their mother's house. They set up one apartment for her and one for them, and they took care of their mother. The brother's wife was a nurse. As her mother-in-law's health gradually declined she was able to take care of her physical needs while their family supported her emotionally. And every year the other brother (and his wife) and their sister (and her husband) alternated taking care of their mother for a week or two so that the caregivers could have a vacation.

Then their mother died. When the will was read it was discovered that, while money and other valuables were to be divided equally, her home had been left solely to the son and daughter-in-law who had taken care of her for so many years. And then, as you've probably guessed by now, the fighting began.

The story isn't unusual. We could each probably write some variation of it ourselves. In fact, it's so common that Jesus used it as an example for the Pharisees and scribes (Lk 15:1–3, 11–32). While our stories may not involve a prodigal son who spends his inheritance foolishly, they almost always include an older brother (or sister, or son-in-law or sister-in-law) who feels cheated out of what should be his or hers. The question isn't really about property at all. The question is about loving, unconditionally.

"Everything I have is yours." These words were spoken, not just to the elder brother in the story, but to the younger as well. These words were spoken to the son and his wife who gave so much of their lives to care for their mother, and to the other children who took care of her for only a week or two every other year. Parents don't keep records, but ungrateful children do. Does your family have a story?

Marriage

"There was a wedding…" (Jn 2:1–11). The daughter of a dear friend of mine is getting married next month. The church and reception hall have been reserved for months; shower and wedding invitations mailed; china and silver patterns registered; final dress and tuxedo fittings scheduled; photographer and caterer hired. It's an exciting time for everyone involved. And all because one young woman and one young man wish to declare publicly that they love each other so much that they want to commit themselves to one another for the rest of their lives.

It was in precisely this setting that Jesus chose to perform his first public miracle. He could have chosen to spin the sun, or to call down fire. Spinning the sun and calling down fire would surely have pointed to the power and glory of God. But Jesus did not choose to point to God's power.

Mary and Jesus were guests at the wedding. Mary noticed the problem first. The wine had run out. The couple would be embarrassed, the guests disappointed, the party ruined. Could Jesus help? "How does your concern affect me?" Of what concern is the wedding of two very ordinary people (we aren't even told their names) in a very ordinary town in Galilee to the God of heaven and earth? And then it happened. Water became wine, and a celebration of human love and commitment became the occasion for the first public miracle of the beloved Son.

The prophet Isaiah uses wedding imagery to reflect the relationship between God and Jerusalem. "You shall be called 'My Delight'…as the bridegroom rejoices over the bride, so shall your God rejoice over you" (Isa 62:1–5).

My friend's daughter's eyes dance these days. She and her fiancé are rarely separated. They have committed themselves to one another and will soon declare their love publicly. Perhaps this is why Jesus chose this human occasion to image God's love for us, not by spinning the sun in the sky but in the committed love of husband and wife right here on earth.

Competition

A little boy sees his brother with an ice cream cone and runs to ask his mother if it's all right to have an ice cream cone before dinner. He really hopes that his mother will take the treat away from his brother, and maybe even scold him in the bargain.

A student pulls out her calculator to solve an exam problem. No sooner does she have the calculator out of her bag than the girl next to her raises her hand to ask the teacher if it is permitted, hoping that she might get a better grade for having pointed out the other girl's infraction.

If the little boy and the teenage student had been sincere in their questions they would have gone directly to the persons involved, wouldn't they? Why, then, rather than address the situation directly, did they choose to go to a higher authority? Could it be that they believed that by making someone else look bad they could make themselves look good? It's a common human failing, I suspect, and not only among children.

The Pharisees knew the law. They knew what had been written regarding divorce. So why did they approach Jesus with the question (Mk 10:2–16)? Perhaps they, too, were hoping to make themselves look good by making someone else look bad. But is that really what God's law is about?

Several years ago a secretary in the office where I was working came to see me about her sister, whose husband routinely beat her. She had encouraged her sister to seek a divorce. However, when her sister asked her pastor if it was permissible for her to divorce her husband, he sternly referred her to this Scripture passage.

The Pharisees wanted Jesus to tell them they were right, but Jesus saw right through them. He described marriage as a covenant, not as a contract; as that sacred union in which a man and a woman are joined together by God as equals, each loving the other as one flesh. God's law is given to protect this reality, not to enforce a contract. Do we understand this? Or do we, like the Pharisees, prefer to use God's law against others in an attempt to make ourselves look good?

Partnership

"To send them out two by two…" (Mk 6:7–13). Over the last couple of weeks my family and I have attended four weddings. Four couples—eight beautiful young people, arriving one by one, sent out two by two. Four weddings—prayers prayed, homilies preached, promises given, blessings bestowed, community sent. Then out of the churches we streamed—gentlemen in tuxedos, bridesmaids radiant in dresses that rivaled the flowers they carried, proud parents and godparents, relatives and friends—and showering the new husband and wife with confetti, popping soap bubbles in the air, we sent them out two by two.

But what, you may ask, does all of this have to do with this Sunday's gospel? What does all of this have to do with sacrament? Why do we Catholic Christians ritualize this very secular act within the context of Scripture and/or Eucharist? Why, when any judge or justice of the peace or ship's captain could legally complete the contract, do we stand before priest or deacon and proclaim covenant?

Perhaps the answer lies in who it is that is being sent and Who it is that is doing the sending. For we believe that this covenant involves, not two, but three; and not just three, but in fact the entire community of faith. Indeed, while they may have been given many shower and wedding gifts, in some subtle way each newly married couple is sent out without any provisions for the journey.

And it is here that we find the true beauty of the sacrament, for in this covenant of love between husband and wife God is also present. It is God, surrounding and sending the newlyweds, Who supports them as their walking stick in the gift of the gathered community. None of us is ever sent out alone. Carrying nothing for the journey reminds us that we must not depend on our own resources. Like the newlyweds, we find the support of God in the sacrament of one another. Husband and wife, newly married couple and community, you and I, called to be God to one another, our God sends us out two by two.

The Good News

Early in the gospel of Mark we read that Jesus is driven by the Spirit "out into the desert…" (Mk 1:12–15). The passage ends with the words "repent and believe in the gospel." Depending upon which formula is used in our parish on Ash Wednesday we may hear these words repeated over and over again. Mark wastes no time in telling us what is expected of us; only twelve verses into his gospel, we are told to "repent and believe" in the Good News.

Jesus is driven out into the desert, among the wild beasts. We may not know about the desert, but we do know how it feels to be in a dangerous place, afraid and alone. We may not know about wild beasts, but we do know about human alienation, and pain, and fear.

In Scripture we often find the word "covenant." We hear that God has entered into a covenant with the people. What is this covenant? Well, first, let's say what covenant is not. A covenant is not a contract. In a contract two parties enter into a legally binding agreement. Covenant is different. A covenant agreement presumes mutual commitment between two parties. And then it gets better because, in this particular covenant, one of the parties is God!

The Good News is that God is not about legality—God is about commitment. God is about commitment to being with us when we feel afraid and alone. God is about commitment to being with us when we feel alienated, when we find ourselves on the outside of the "in" crowd or on the just, but less popular, side of an ethical issue. God is about commitment to being with us when we suffer the pain of loss—the death of a loved one, the loss of our health, or of our job. God is about commitment to being with us in the desert and to sending angels to minister to us when we face the wild beasts. This is the incredible Good News that Mark is telling us to believe!

Unfortunately, we don't always keep our side of the covenant agreement. Sometimes we turn away and choose to walk in the desert alone—insisting on doing it our own way. Sometimes we ignore God's voice, preferring to make our decisions based on other voices. Sometimes we make bad choices. We fail to keep our part of the covenant. But this covenant-that-is-not-a-contract cannot be broken and, no matter what we do, our God will never turn away from us.

This is the Good News! This is the covenant our God has made with us. We have only to repent—and believe.

CHAPTER 8

A Golden Parachute...

There is a place in each of us—
A firm and holy place.

Located down so deep within our heart
that no amount of searching there
can ever find it out—
This firm and holy place.

No matter how the winds may blow,
it's our magnetic pole and holds us fast—
This firm and holy place.

The sand may shift around our feet,
but standing on this rock
we stand secure—
This firm and holy place.

It's like the midnight or the noon
around which all the hours of day revolve—
a wellspring and a waterfall,
a source and spending
of the energy of life—
This firm and holy place.

But we must each this treasure seek ourselves.
For nowhere is it written on a map,
no guidebook written in the stars
can lead us to—
This firm and holy place.

So hold secure and know that as it's promised—so it is.

In each of us the Potter breathes his love
and seals it deep as ocean's deep
and high as sky is high.

Within our darkness and our light,
each part of us is formed to hold this prize—
This firm and holy place.

I originally called this poem "A Centering." It was one of the first poems I ever had published, and it speaks to me of a reality that I can't express in any other way than in poetry. It's a poem about faith—about our belief that there is some spark of the Divine in each one of us that cannot, will not, be denied.

Looking back on the piece in the context of the workplace it strikes me that this faith—this spark of the Divine—is really a kind of spiritual "golden parachute." This is the "guarantee," the "retirement plan," the "package" that we can count on to be there when we need it. In business a golden parachute can be an incentive to keep working or an insurance plan for when one retires. Having a golden parachute means having something to count on if one's position is eliminated, or in the event the corporation encounters operational or financial difficulties. In other words, in business a golden parachute becomes a kind of "firm and holy place"—if business happens to be our religion.

But business is not (or should not be!) our religion. The golden parachute that business promises is fine—as far as it goes. But the golden parachute that the Divine promises is without limit. Why is this so difficult for us to accept? Why is it so much easier to accept that a corporation can offer security than it is to accept the security our God offers?

The golden parachute that God promises isn't something written on paper and filed away in some musty file cabinet; it's God's own Spirit burning in our deepest center. The golden parachute that God promises isn't something we have to look forward to in some distant future; it's the kingdom of God in our midst—right here, right now. The golden parachute that God promises isn't something we may or may not actually receive, depending on whether or not we're still with the company (or whether or not we live long enough to take advantage of it!). This golden parachute is promised to us from all eternity and is ours today, if we will only claim it.

This golden parachute is God—our Creator, our Redeemer, our Sanctifier—our "firm and holy place."

...For Statesmen

Enthusiasm—from the Greek *en*, meaning in, and *theo*, meaning God—can thus be defined as having God within. An enthusiastic person is one who experiences the presence of an indwelling God.

Picture someone you know that you would characterize as being enthusiastic. Chances are it will be someone who isn't afraid to exhibit emotion, someone who is comfortable expressing deep feeling and caring. The word itself implies some strong affection for that about which one is enthusiastic. Think of the young skater or gymnast practicing tirelessly day after day, or the new college graduate or intern spending long hours developing new skills. They exhibit enthusiasm. Picture a group of children playing baseball, or a kitten with a ball of yarn. Enthusiasm seems to come naturally to the young.

"I am come that you may have life, life in abundance" (Jn 10:10). What is this life in abundance of which Jesus speaks? He directs the apostles to let the children approach, "for the kingdom of God belongs to such as these" (Mt 19:13–15). What is it about the children that the kingdom of God should belong to them? Could it be their enthusiasm? Could it be their recognition of an indwelling God that assures life?

Emerson said: "Nothing great was ever achieved without enthusiasm." Great financiers; great inventors; great statesmen: these are some examples of people of great enthusiasm, people we hold up and emulate. Often, as in the case of the late UN Secretary-General Däg Hammarskjöld, when we look more closely at the lives of great men and women we find that it was their relationship with this indwelling God that sparked their creativity and energy, that fueled their enthusiasm.

Can we say as much? If we lack enthusiasm about our work, is it because our work is meaningless? Or could it be that we have forgotten Who it is that blesses and gives meaning to our work, inviting us to participate as co-creators of the kingdom?

Where, in our lives, do we recognize the presence of the indwelling God? Where is our enthusiasm?

...For Builders

At the close of the second millennium there was an increased interest in the Book of Revelation. The air was thick with dire predictions of everything from aliens to Armageddon. And many people were afraid.

Actually, the Book of Revelation isn't about fear but, rather, about Jesus and hope (Rev 21:9–28). There is a city surrounded by a wall, but built into the wall are many gates opening out in all directions to all peoples. There is no temple in the city, no distinction based on style of worship; in this city the temple is the Lord. There are no rolling blackouts in this city; it gleams with the radiance of God.

The beautiful images describe a place of beauty and peace, yet people persist in finding fear there. True, in other sections there are images that are not so peaceful, reflecting the experience of the Christian communities for which the book was written. These images, many taken from the Hebrew Scriptures, may appear strange to us, but they were familiar to John's intended audience. Christians were being persecuted by Rome. Messages had to be written in language that the oppressors could not understand, a kind of "code." What evolved was, in fact, written to reassure, not to frighten.

"My peace I give to you...do not let your hearts be...afraid" (Jn 14:27). Words of reassurance. But the early Christian community was not peaceful. Even then there were conflicting ideas about what one must do in order to be saved. Were they to "keep the rules" or "love one another"? There was conflict. Walls were being raised up. The beautiful city was receding into memory.

But it doesn't have to end that way. The vision of the beautiful city is real. Jesus is its cornerstone. We are its builders. What it will finally look like is up to us. Will we build walls to keep others out, or will we open wide the gates of invitation? Will we impose rules and dispense fear, or will we rule with love and gift with peace? The time of revelation may be in the future, but the future is now.

...For Financial Planners

"What's all this about 'sheep'? We're not 'sheep', and we resent being compared to sheep! By the way, what's the latest on high tech stocks? Do you think day trading is really a good idea? Have you invested in a high resolution TV yet?"

Conversations around the water cooler or in the chat room. Voices vying for our attention, calling us to follow—like sheep. Radio and TV. Newspaper and network. Listen and you can almost hear the bleating. At this beginning of the twenty-first century it would seem that Bill Gates is the new shepherd and Microsoft is the gate, and anyone trying to enter with a Mac need not apply!

"Save yourselves from this corrupt generation" (Acts 2:40). Perhaps Peter wouldn't say it quite that way today, but the question is just as true today as it was then. Do we get the point? It's a matter of *faith*. Sometimes we seem to be wandering all over the place, something of which no self-respecting sheep would ever be guilty. We might not want to be compared to sheep but at least sheep know which gate leads to safety and which to harm—and they know which voice to listen to when they're confused and lost.

In these days of conflicts and wars, of inflation and recession, of genetic engineering and death with dignity, we find ourselves drowning in a cacophony of voices calling from every direction. Which voice do we listen to? By which gate do we enter?

...For Members of the Board

"When...the doors of the house where the disciples had met were locked for fear..." (Jn 20:19). Sounds like a conference room somewhere in downtown Chicago! The disciples, that first "board of directors" is meeting, but they don't know what to do—and they're afraid. So they've locked the doors.

What were they afraid of? Scripture says "fear of the Jews." But what kind of sense does *that* make? These people *are* Jews, yet here they sit, afraid of their own people. Why?

Perhaps it's because, having walked with Jesus, they know that they are "different," but they're not sure what that will mean. They have been exposed to a new way of being; there are new expectations. A new "law," a new "mission statement" if you will, has come to replace the old, but they lack direction—and they're afraid.

Today, while the circumstances may have changed, for many of us the fear remains. Like those early disciples we sit in our conference rooms with the doors locked, afraid of our own shadows (our shadow is, after all, a part of who we are). We wait for someone to come in to tell us what to do, and then we lock the doors to keep them out! We look for direction, but we close our ears. Paralyzed by our fear we talk to ourselves in little locked rooms meant to keep us safe but which, in reality, only serve to keep us isolated.

Do we believe that Jesus is in our midst, whether it's in the conference room or the operating room, the factory or the shop? Do we believe that, as he did for the apostles on that first Pentecost, Jesus has breathed his Spirit on each one of us? Are we open to this Gift that has come into our lives? Or do we continue to lock the door in fear and then wonder why no one can come in?

...For Employers

I have a hunch that John's gospel about the hired man (Jn 10:11–18) could lead to some interesting family discussions. My parents grew up in an age when an individual took a job, expecting to work with that employer for most of his or her life and eventually retire with a farewell party and a gold watch. My children, on the other hand, have no particular loyalty to their employers and fully expect to move from job to job, hopefully improving their salary and position with each change and finally retiring with a sizable retirement package. And, as callous as it may sound, the truth is that today's employers have few illusions about employee loyalty either.

Recently I have begun to see articles about new benefits being offered as employee incentives. A "corporate concierge" will take care of dropping off your cleaning or even picking up a birthday gift for your spouse. On-site day care is increasingly available. Flex-hours are becoming the norm. Employers, it seems, are beginning to feel the pinch of a job market where the employee calls the shots.

John's gospel talks about a deeply committed employer and a less-than-committed employee. The first, the good shepherd, knows his sheep and is so personally committed to them that he offers the ultimate benefit—he lays down his life for them. The hired man, on the other hand, only cares about what he's being paid. He is committed to nothing but his own salary and position. His attitude is, "What's in it for me?"

Each of us has a vocation, a work we are called to do. For most of us our vocation is lived out in the world as workers and tenders of the home. We are single adults, wives and husbands; we are doctors and lawyers, students and service workers. We are the sheep for whom the Good Shepherd has laid down his life. We are called to continue to build up the kingdom, to live the gospel in the world as God's very own sons and daughters. Are we committed to our call? Or are we more like the hired man who runs away at the first sight of the wolf?

...For Soldiers and Saints

In May we celebrate both Memorial Day and the feast of St. Joan of Arc. Since Joan of Arc is my patron saint I probably spend more time thinking about her than other people might. Over the years I have come to see her as many things: as a saint, as a strong young woman who heard God's call to action, and as a martyr who laid down her life in faith so that her people—the people of France—might be free. Until recently, however, I never really thought of Joan as a veteran. Yet that's precisely what she was. Joan was a soldier who lost her life by fighting for her country and for her faith. Joan of Arc, like so many others before and after her, gave her life because she believed in peace.

But what, you may ask, does this have to do with us? Well, every Sunday we gather as a free people, free to worship our God, free to live in a land where justice and peace prevail. Others before us have given their lives so that we might enjoy this freedom. But when we return to our offices and workplaces, our homes, our classrooms, our shops and our factories, we sometimes find ourselves confronted by people who don't stand for the same things we stand for. We may find ourselves imprisoned by prejudice or smothered by economic inequality. We may feel trapped in the hopelessness of a job that feeds our body but starves our spirit, or pressured to make decisions based on voices that say we have to make a profit, even if it's at the cost of human dignity. We may find ourselves in the position of having to fight for what we believe in.

Standing up for what we believe in can be hard—so hard, in fact, that we may not believe we can do it alone. The Good News is that we don't have to! Jesus promised that, even when we feel weak and vulnerable, even if we face death itself, we won't be alone. Jesus has sent the Paraclete, the Holy Spirit, to be with us (Jn 20:21–22).

And that's not all. Every Sunday, when we leave Church to go our separate ways, we go in the sure knowledge that all the holy men and women who have gone before us, all those who have laid down their lives so that we might be free, go with us. Every Sunday we are reminded that we walk with the entire Communion of Saints. Every Sunday, then, becomes a kind of Memorial Day. Go in peace…

…For Farmers

Most of us are familiar with the New Testament accounts of the multiplication of loaves and fishes, such as the one we find in the gospel of John (6:1–15). But many of us are unaware that there are stories of miraculous feedings in the Old Testament as well. In fact, many gospel events parallel similar stories from the Hebrew Scriptures. In light of this fact, then, why are we so skeptical about the possibility that such things continue to happen today? Take the story of the multiplication of loaves as an example. Because of advances in the science of agriculture farmers today are able to produce far more usable grain than was possible in even the recent past. Consequently, the amount of food that can be provided has been multiplied many times over.

Jesus predicted that those who followed him would do what He had done and even greater things. We are able to count the healing stories in the Scriptures, but the number of persons who are healed every day thanks to new discoveries in the field of medicine are countless. People are brought back, literally, from the dead as hearts are stopped and then restarted during surgery. And the examples go on and on.

But the gospel stories don't stop with miracles. There is something else going on as well. The writer of John's gospel says "Jesus took the loaves, *gave thanks*, and *distributed* them...." Do we *give thanks* for the miracles of modern medicine? Do we attribute to God the gift of the human intellect? Do we recognize our need for rain and sun to reap the gifts of the earth? Do we remember the connection between what we do and what God has done for us?

Miracles don't occur only in the Scriptures; miracles are happening every day, all around us. God continues to heal the sick, to give sight to the blind, and to raise the dead. God continues to recognize our hunger and to give us what we need to be fed. But we must also do our part. We live in a country of incredible abundance. Do we distribute the good things we are given to share? Do we remember to give thanks for all the miracles in our lives?

...For Healthcare Workers

When I was in high school in Chicago I took the elevated train to school every morning with one of my classmates. This girl, who was a friend of mine, had a speech defect. Born with a cleft palate, her speech was somewhat guttural and difficult to understand. For most of us who knew her this posed no problem, but while she was growing up there were those who had teased and made fun of her. Consequently, she had always been somewhat shy and withdrawn around people she didn't know.

A year ago I was attending a breakfast meeting and found myself sitting across from an attractive woman my age. As we talked over coffee she told me that she was in marketing and that she had started her own business a few years earlier. Somehow we got around to talking about where we had gone to school and I was surprised and delighted to find that the shy teenager I had known in high school had grown into this gracious and confident woman. Doctors had been able to correct the defect and speech therapy had helped her to overcome her shyness. It truly seemed like a miracle.

In John's gospel we hear Jesus say "the one who believes in me will also do the works that I do and, in fact, will do greater works than these" (Jn 14:12). I doubt that the surgeons and therapists who healed my friend thought of what they were doing as "miraculous." They were just human beings doing their job, nothing out of the ordinary, all in a day's work. The surgery was routine, the therapy that which was usually indicated for this condition.

"They brought to him a man who had an impediment in his speech..." (Mk 7:32–37). What Jesus did was nothing out of the ordinary. It was a human hand that reached out and touched the man; human spittle that healed him. Jesus believed that God worked through him. I believe that God worked through the hands of my friend's surgeons. In fact, I believe that all the work we do bears God's fingerprints. Jesus promised that this would be so. Do we believe what he told us? Do we recognize the miraculous in the ordinary work of our human hands?

...For Hospice Workers

A few months ago my husband and I happened to catch the second part of a four-part television series. The subject of the series was death or, more specifically, the end of life. The first program in the series had dealt with the growing availability of hospice care and the people who provide it. On this particular night the topic under discussion was palliative care as a growing medical specialty.

In many cases it can be difficult to tell which the doctor is more concerned about, the person or the disease. Unfortunately, doctors sometimes seem unable or unwilling to admit the necessity of suffering and death. While taking careful notes on a patient's vital signs, they may not even think to ask about his or her pain. Death has become the enemy. To "lose" a patient to death is seen as somehow shameful, and when a patient dies it is as though the doctor feels that he or she has failed.

Happily, today there is growing concern for treating the human spirit as well as the body. Patients' rights advocates are negotiating with insurance companies to cover the costs of hospice care, attendants for patients who need twenty-four-hour care, and new medications that help to eliminate pain, thus allowing patients to enter into their own dying process with peace and dignity.

Isaiah describes the suffering servant as one who enters into suffering without shame (50:4–7). Jesus reminds us that it is only by facing death that we can overcome it. There is no shame in dying. Dying is simply a part of living. Their faith in the dignity of life allows hospice care professionals and specialists in palliative care to attend to the needs of the dying. They do not struggle against death. Instead, they choose to accompany those who might otherwise be left to die alone. Theirs are not mere pious words, but works born of deep faith in the value of human life.

...For the Unprepared

"If only I had known then what I know now!" How often have we heard that said? Or even said it ourselves? "If I had known, I would have done differently. But I was afraid...."

In the course of our lives we are called upon to make many decisions, perhaps hundreds of them every day. What time should we get up? What clothes should we wear? Which train do we catch? Which flavor of coffee should we order? black or with cream? bagel or muffin? And that's before we even get to work!

But there are other questions, questions like: what kind of work would

I enjoy and be good at? Where do I go to get another job if I lose the one I have? What happens if Social Security isn't there when I need it? How can I manage to work and, at the same time, take care of my aging parents? What if I become ill or incapacitated? These questions are tougher. These are questions about the unexpected. These questions remind us that, no matter how we try to prepare, no matter what stocks we invest in or what insurance policies we buy, there are things over which we have no control. These questions frighten us.

Luke talks about being ready, being prepared for the unexpected. "The Son of Man is coming at an unexpected hour" (Lk 12:35–40). He talks about being caught unaware in the middle of the night. These are unsettling situations. Perhaps that's why Luke starts out by having Jesus say, "Do not be afraid." But who wouldn't be afraid? What is Luke trying to say?

To find our answer let's look again at some of the tough questions we talked about earlier. Jesus tells us that the Son of Man will come when we least expect him—when we're least prepared. What are some of the things we're not prepared for? Maybe it's when we've lost our job and the insurance benefits have run out. Maybe the darkest part of the night is when our health, or that of someone we love, is failing and the doctors say there's nothing more they can do.

Abraham and Sarah had given up hope of ever bearing a child. Later, they faced the possible death of their only son, Isaac. Maybe we're having difficulty conceiving. Maybe we're facing an unexpected pregnancy. Maybe we're being called upon to endure the death of a child from trauma or disease. No one is ever prepared for this kind of life-shattering experience.

And then we hear Jesus saying, "Do not be afraid." We hear a story about a master who arrives unannounced, who promises to come when we least expect him. Could it be that that's not such a bad thing after all? Could it be that that's the treasure?

Maybe the Good News is that, if we will just let go and trust this God of surprises rather than trying to control everything ourselves, we will be given what we need precisely when we need it. While the tough questions may not go away we won't have to face them alone because it is then, right when things seem darkest, that our God of surprises will arrive. We just need to be wide-awake and ready for him when he arrives. Then, when God knocks, all we'll have to do is open the door…

...For the Wealthy

There are people among us, even in religious circles, who would say that being rich and happy are signs of God's favor, while being poor or ill are signs that one has found disfavor with God. (Job suffered from similar presumptions on the part of the people of his day.) Luke's gospel contradicts this kind of thinking. In the so-called Sermon on the Plain (Lk 6:17, 20–26), Luke, unlike Matthew in his Sermon on the Mount (5:3–12), speaks specifically about *physical* hunger and destitution, not *spiritual*. This gospel challenges everything that our consumer society tells us with regard to possessions and success.

But does that mean that someone who is successful is somehow wrong? Is it bad to have it good? Perhaps Jeremiah can help us out here. "Cursed are those who trust in mere mortals..." (Jer 17:5–8). Jeremiah doesn't talk about what one has but about where one places his or her trust. The question seems to be less about what we have than about what we are willing to risk if justice demands it. What happens if we are challenged to take an ethical stand that may mean losing financial or economic status? Do we buy into the thinking that says, "Don't rock the boat"? How do we respond?

Luke's gospel isn't really about being hopeless so much as it is about being without hope. Do we have sufficient faith to stick to our convictions, even if doing so means that others may hate and insult us? Do we have hope in a God who loves us, or is our hope based on the latest Dow Jones numbers? When news commentators talk about a recession does the word move us to consider its consequences for millions of persons adversely affected by an out-of-balance global economy? Or do we think only of its impact on our own checkbook? Do we value a strong economy over a strong character? Do we believe that someone can be blessed, even if he or she is poor? Or do we believe it is a curse to be hungry?

Our currency bears the affirmation "In God We Trust." Do we really believe that?

...For People of Faith

"I've worked hard. I deserve a raise. My boss had better come up with something good or I'm out of here."

"My boss told me to take all the time off I needed when my mother died. I'd do just about anything for her. She's been really good to me."

Two employees; two situations; two responses.

In the first situation the employee has worked hard. Historically, he knows his boss to be a just man. The employee has always been paid fairly, but he feels he has earned more. His faith rests squarely on his own efforts and looks for a response from his boss.

In the second situation the employee knows, because of personal experience, that her boss will listen and understand her needs. She has faith in her boss and recognizes that she has received more than she could ever hope to deserve on her own merits. This employee, then, is moved to respond out of gratitude for all that she has received.

""A certain creditor had two debtors..." (Lk 7:41–50). Faith does not exist in a vacuum. It requires an "object"—be it a person (the boss? oneself?), a thing (stock portfolio? a degree?), an ideology (a political system? religion?), or, perhaps, an institution (the state? the Church?) for us to have faith *in*. The first employee places his faith in himself. The second employee places her faith in her boss. And each of these may be valid. But Jesus calls us to go deeper, to become a "people of faith," relying solely on the power of God.

"Lord, increase our faith." Where is your golden parachute? In what do you put your faith? In whom do you trust? Look at your response. The answer may surprise you.

CHAPTER 9

We're Pregnant...

This is the prayer I pray for you
this Advent season.
A prayer that you might find—
not only "Christ"
in Christmastime—
but *"time."*

It is a prayer I pray with you in darkness.
A prayer that we
might take the *time*
to walk in Light.

Time—to hear the crunch our feet make in the snow—
and not just time
to shovel it away.

Time—to hear the words of Christmas carols—
and *time* to mean
the whispered words we pray.

The prayer I pray for you with all my heart,
and ask that you please
pray for me
these Advent days,
is that, for just a moment, we
might come away
and know the peace
of Christ
in Christmas*time.*

Does anyone ever have enough time? I knew I certainly didn't. And since I was pretty sure that most of the people I knew were having the same problem this seemed like the perfect Christmas gift—the gift of *time*.

My husband and I were visiting friends in Wisconsin. We were driving north on County Road 22 when we were surprised to see truckloads of Christmas trees heading south. It seemed so early! It was, after all, only the day after Thanksgiving. At this rate Christmas trees would be popping up on corner lots (and in living rooms) all over town before we had a chance to say "Tannenbaum"! And then it hit me—today was the unofficial opening day of the secular season known as "[fill in the blank] shopping days 'til Christmas."

As I prepared to enter the busyness of it all something inside of me wanted to scream. I just couldn't face the prospect of doing it all again. I wasn't ready. I didn't have *time* for all of this! I didn't have *time* to bake cookies and make lists and go shopping and wrap presents and clean house and put up the tree and hang the garland and entertain guests and...and...and... And that's when I wrote the poem.

Maybe it was the words as they tumbled out onto the paper. Maybe it was the process of writing itself. Or maybe it was the prayer. Whatever it was, somewhere along the line I felt the tension slipping away. Christmas shoppers weren't the only ones counting the days until Christmas. There was another season coming, a sacred season, the season of Advent.

For four weeks we would prepare for Christmas and the celebration, again, of that moment when the Divine entered so intimately into human history that there could never again be any separation between the sacred and the secular. This was not just a time of preparation—this was a time of gestation, a time of pregnancy. Advent isn't something we prepare for; it's something that happens to us. We can struggle and fuss or we can take the time to enjoy the experience. The choice is ours. But, either way, Christmas will come—and the Baby will arrive—all in God's good *time*.

...With Healing Gifts

The other day I saw an interesting photo of a new General Motors product. No, it's not a more fuel-efficient car. Nor is it a new kind of vehicle using gyroscopes to move forward or backward as the user "thinks" about moving. You won't find this product in an automobile showroom, and it probably won't make the evening news. But to some it is a miracle. This conveyance allows men and women who have lost limbs to leprosy to move about independently. While it cannot cure their bodies, it can restore their dignity.

And there are other miracles. One thing we do hear about on TV is laser eye surgery. As one who has worn glasses for nearsightedness since childhood I can appreciate what a gift it would be to wake up in the morning able to see without fumbling for glasses or fussing with contact lenses. And just last week I heard that researchers have pinpointed the area of the brain that translates vibrations into sound. This research may one day restore hearing to individuals suffering nerve damage to the inner ear.

"[T]the blind receive their sight, the lame walk, the lepers are cleansed, the deaf hear..." (Mt 11:2–11). Isaiah foretold great things (Isa 35:1–6A, 10). John the Baptist pointed to Jesus as that One in whom these things had come to pass. We read Scripture stories of Jesus' miraculous healings and wish that we could have been there. We travel great distances to visit the places where we are told miracles are taking place. "What [do we] go out to the desert to see?" What new signs do we seek?

Advent is a pregnant time. We wait patiently for the miracle of Christmas, the birth of God's own Son. But too often, after the last cookie has been eaten and the last decorations put away, we forget. We go back to "business as usual" and we miss the miracles that continue to happen every day. Isaiah told us what the kingdom would look like. We just have to open our eyes. Who knows, maybe what we're looking for is right there on the evening news...

...With Cautious Hope

Christmas shopping. Market researchers tell us that, while traffic is up, sales are down. Manufacturers and retailers are looking forward to this holiday shopping season with cautious hopefulness. There is caution because, since the events of September 11, 2001, many people have suffered a loss of income that could force them to cut back on spending. On the other hand, many are hopeful that sales will be good, believing that people may actually increase their gift spending out of a feeling of gratitude and relief at having survived the terrorist attacks.

Store owners are reacting to these uncertain times in a variety of ways. For example, some stores that normally hire additional help during the holidays have decided not to do so this year. Instead, they are choosing to rely on their regular employees to work more hours, should the need arise. They are, you might say, planning for the worst while expecting the best, acting cautiously but with the hope that their caution will prove unnecessary.

During the season of Advent our Scripture readings reflect a similar mood of cautious hopefulness. "Keep awake...be ready..." (Mt 24:37–44). Matthew's gospel brings to mind events at the terrorist attack sites. "Two men will be [working in the building]; one will be taken, and one will be left." We've heard stories of people who survived—and of people who didn't. Were they ready? Are we? Do we get up every morning prepared for the coming of the "master of the house"?

How is it that we can be so good at preparing for the economic repercussions of what is going on in the world around us and, at the same time, be so bad about hearing the wake-up call they represent? The clerks at the mall recognize their responsibility to be ready for whatever the market, or their employer, might ask of them. Are we as ready as they are? Each time we begin a new liturgical year we find, if we are looking for it, much cause for hope. "You know what time it is...it is now the moment for you to wake from sleep" (Rom 13:11). Are you ready?

...With Joyful Hearts

Gaudete, the Latin word for "rejoice." "Shout for joy!" "Rejoice in the Lord always!" The Third Sunday in Advent is called "Gaudete Sunday." Purple vestments are replaced by rose. The penitential feeling of the season lifts (Advent was once more like Lent then than it is today) and we rejoice.

Not much has changed in the last fifty years or so about the way we wait for Christmas. In anticipation of Christmas, bell-ringers still greet shoppers on street corners, and children still wait to sit on Santa's lap. Dads still spend hours putting toys together (although today the toys are likely to be computerized), and Moms still spend weeks baking cookies and addressing cards. Christmas trees still appear overnight on corner lots, only to be carried off and to reappear in living rooms, festooned with lights and shiny decorations.

The people in Jesus' time weren't all that different (Lk 3:15–18). Then as now, the people were waiting for Christmas (although they didn't know about "Christmas" yet; they only knew they were waiting for the Messiah). They came to John to ask what kind of preparations they should make. John could have told them to go and wait "in the church," but he didn't. No, John instructed the people to prepare for the Messiah right where they were. They were working people (and not all in particularly well-respected professions, at that). John told them to do their work differently in anticipation of the One who was to come. They were to work in such a way that it would serve the good and bring joy to the world.

You see, that's where Christmas happens. Christmas happens on factory floors and in shopping malls, in crowded diners and in lonely hospital rooms. Christmas happens wherever and whenever one person opens his or her heart to another. So rejoice and be glad—in your work and in your play. Sing joyfully, renewed in God's love, for "the Lord, your God, is in your midst" (Zeph 3:14–18A). Look around. The Messiah has come. In fact, he may be sitting right next to you...

...With Expectations of "What Should Be"

"Life is difficult." Scott Peck's words at the beginning of his work, *The Road Less Traveled*, should come as no surprise to most of us. And yet they do, especially at this time of year. Family members become ill. Friends lose their jobs. Suicide numbers go up. Crimes against children continue. "It wasn't supposed to be this way."

The Scriptures speak of two people who have expectations of how things are "supposed to be." King David, concerned because the ark of God dwells in a tent while he lives in a fine house, proposes to build a "house" for God (2 Sam 7:1–5). But God does not need a house of cedar. God has other plans.

An angel appears to a virgin (Lk 1:26–38). She will conceive and bear a child who will be called the Son of God. Israel looks for a warrior king. God enters the world as a tiny, helpless baby. "It wasn't supposed to be this way."

It is natural to have expectations about how Christmas is "supposed" to be. Unfortunately, sometimes what we expect and what actually happens are two very different things. David had plans to build a house for God. A virgin named Mary had plans to marry the man to whom she was betrothed. Each had expectations of how life was "supposed to be." But God had other plans. The house of David would be greater than anything David could ever have imagined. And God's own Son would be born because of the willingness of a virgin to say "Yes."

It isn't easy to give up control, even when we know the eventual outcome of our decisions. It's even more difficult to give up control when we have no idea what will happen. It demands "faith," the belief that God knows how life is "supposed" to be—and the willingness to say "Yes." It's what God asked of David—and of Mary. It's what God asks of each one of us...

...With Hungry Longing

As the Church approaches the end of Advent we find that while, technically, we are still waiting for Christmas, even our Scripture readings anticipate the birth of Christ. Christmas is like that, here—but not yet. It is in this same spirit of anticipation that I wrote this Christmas poem. Like Advent itself, it begins…

In Darkness

A point of light
in a velvet sky.
A Word whispered
to a waiting world.

A virgin conceives;
the universe gives birth.
A carpenter dreams
and all creation
rises from its slumber.

A sleeping Child wakes the dawn.
The sun bows down
before the star.

Laid in a manger,
the Babe becomes bread
and hunger
is
no more.

...With Possibility

As I walk over to St. Peter's Church from the train station in downtown Chicago I pass a construction site. At first it was just a big hole in the ground. Nothing seemed to be going on. Then they built a pedestrian walkway, and signs went up around the area. Things were starting to happen.

That's much like what we hear in the Scriptures. Isaiah tells us what signs to look for—a voice crying out, highways where there were none, valleys filled in, mountains made low, and rugged land that becomes a plain (Isa 40:1–5). Signs will go up around the area. Things will start to happen.

Then John appears on the scene (we haven't heard much about him since the Visitation), not just as baptizer but as messenger (Mk 1:1–8). It seems he has two jobs—to welcome those who come to him for baptism, and to witness to the One who is to come. His clothing is distinctive, as foretold in the Hebrew Scriptures. He witnesses with his life. Signs are going up around the area. Things are starting to happen.

As I walk over to St. Peter's down Madison Street from the train station I pass a construction site. But perhaps that mass of steel and pipe isn't the only construction site I pass. What about all those people on their way to work? Aren't we all under construction? As we walk to our jobs in the Loop aren't we also called to those other two jobs? Like John, aren't we also called to welcome back those who have been away, to accept without judgment? Like John, aren't we also called to witness with our lives to the One who is to come?

Conversion is a process, just like that building over on Madison Street. It doesn't happen overnight. Francis of Assisi heard a voice saying, "Rebuild my church." That same voice is speaking to us. Do we hear it? Are we paying attention? God calls us to rebuild the church, the people of God, who are under construction. God calls us to be the signs, to witness with our lives to the One whose coming we prepare to celebrate, again—and still—and not yet.

The site is ready. Let the construction begin...

...With Dawning Awareness

Christmas Light

As light enters day
the Son of Man rises
like a star in the east—
and a Baby cries.

From the other side of time
a clock strikes;
the curtain of night is parted—
and Day is born.

Shepherds shake the darkness
from their cloaks;
an Infant nurses
at its mother's breast—
and we are fed.

...With Yearning in the Darkness

The skies over our city are noticeably brighter these days. A long, mild autumn invited neighbors to decorate trees with miles of colored bulbs and to line driveways with electric candles. Icicle lights, crystal strands of blue and white, drip from rooftops. Red and green stoplights flash a counterpoint to streetlights dressed in green and red garland. Almost everywhere one drives, there is light. Almost everywhere, but not quite.

Late yesterday evening, driving home from a meeting in a nearby town in misting rain and dropping temperatures, I realized just how dark the darkness can be. I turned on my brights but they did little to illuminate the narrow ribbon of highway ahead. I found myself straining to see the Christmas lights as I passed a farmhouse here or a small subdivision there.

Traveling in darkness can be frightening. There is an inky quality to the night sky that seems to absorb the light. It is the inky color of Advent, and with fear lurking only just beneath the surface we strain to see light.

John the Baptist was an Advent figure (Mt 3:1–12). He lived at a time of much darkness on the earth. People came to him looking for light. To those who searched with a pure heart he foretold the coming of a Light brighter than their wildest imaginings. But not all came with pure hearts. John was not fooled by the Pharisees and Sadducees. They asked for light, but John saw the darkness in their hearts. They were the "politically correct" of their day and the light they sought was like an electric candle on the driveway, a flame without fire.

Advent nights are long. We decorate our homes in anticipation of Christmas Light. But are we ready to risk the heat of such a Flame? Or do we prefer glass icicles that burn without melting? Are we willing to risk entering the darkness and become one with the people who "have seen a great light" (Isa 9:1–6)? Or do we prefer the cool safety of electric candles that can be packed away in the basement when Christmas is over?

…With Humble Acceptance

Whether it's the Fourth Sunday of Advent or the Fourth of July, technically we are still waiting for Christmas. But as the calendar edges closer to December 24 our thoughts naturally turn toward the birth of Christ. Here in the Midwest where I live our waiting begins much like a December night, with snow and a cold wind…

In the Stillness

A crisp, cold wind—
A silvery light.
A crust of snow—
A starry night.

A gentle knock—
A harsh reply.
A humble stall—
A baby's cry.

An angel's song—
A curtain torn.
A virgin's "Yes"—
A Child is born.

Jesus is knocking at the door of our heart, seeking a place to be born. Can we offer our lives, humble as they are? Two thousand years ago Mary said "Yes" and Elizabeth rejoiced that what had been spoken by the Lord had been fulfilled (Lk 1:39–45). The curtain of separation between God and humankind had been torn away, and in the stillness the long-awaited kingdom of God had come—a kingdom here, but not yet.

...With a New Way of Being

Baptism, and a new way of seeing.

Shortly after Christmas we celebrate the Baptism of the Lord. In Mark's gospel we read: "just as he was coming up out of the water, he saw the heavens torn apart and the Spirit descending like a dove on him. And a voice came from heaven, 'You are my Son, the Beloved'" (1:10–11). New ways of seeing, and of being seen.

During the weeks prior to Christmas it seemed that lights were popping up everywhere—festooning neighborhood tress, dripping off suburban roofs, bouncing off the walls of towering skyscrapers. What a wonderful metaphor for the light of Christ! But now what? Almost overnight the lights have disappeared. If, indeed, the light of Christ has come into the world, why does it suddenly feel so dark?

At baptism each of us was given a candle, a symbol of the light of Christ. It was as though the Church, preparing us for the darkness we would face, offered us light and a new way of seeing. In the Scriptures we hear Isaiah inviting us, like a mother, to quench our thirst, to "Come, buy wine and milk without money and without price" (Isa 55:1). In a society that says you get what you pay for, this is not the way we are used to seeing things. In 1 John we hear that whoever "is born of God conquers the world" (5:4). As citizens of what is arguably the strongest military power in the world, these words seem very strange. As citizens of the kingdom of God, however, they make perfect sense.

In baptism we, like Jesus, have become God's beloved sons and daughters, citizens of God's kingdom. As children of God, we too are called to see the world differently. But now the Christmas lights have been packed away, and winter darkness again threatens to overcome us. "How are we to see?" we ask. Well, maybe this would be a good time to light our baptismal candle...

...With New Questions

In the readings of Advent, we hear John the Baptist saying, "It's not about me" (or words to that effect). He must have posed quite a strange figure for the Jerusalem Jews to send their priests and Levites to ask him, "Who are you?" (Jn 1:19). In fact, I think that John the Baptist must have looked a little bit like Santa Claus.

Don't misunderstand. I do realize that Santa Claus wears a red suit (as opposed to camel's hair) and has white whiskers. But that doesn't make Santa any less of a strange figure, if you think about it. In fact, when my daughter was three years old she was so afraid of Santa that she wouldn't go near him! That is, until she figured out that Christmas wasn't about Santa at all. No, when she got to be four my daughter figured out that Christmas was about her!

That lasted for another two or three years. But then a marvelous thing happened. My daughter began to realize that Christmas wasn't about her, either. That was when she began to understand about Jesus. Oh, sure, the Nativity set with Mary and Joseph and the baby Jesus had been a part of every Christmas of her life. But it wasn't until then that she started to make the connection. That's when she began to notice that other people got presents, too, and that she could give presents as well as receive them.

Somewhere in the midst of all the "why" questions she asked, "Why do we give presents to people at Christmas?" and "What does Santa Claus have to do with it?" And then she started to understand. As John the Baptist explains to his questioners in John's gospel, it really isn't about him. Do we understand what John the Baptist was saying? Or, like my three-year-old daughter, are we still looking for Santa Claus?

...With Gifts and Treasures

"Behold, a State Street merchant, a LaSalle Street lawyer, and a doctor from Presbyterian St. Luke's arrived at St. Peter's Church in downtown Chicago asking, 'Where is the newborn king of the Jews?'"

No, Matthew didn't put it quite that way, but isn't that pretty much what happened (Mt 2:1–12)? Gifts of gold (precious metal and means of exchange), frankincense (symbol of priests and protectors of the law) and myrrh (symbol of human life and death)—are these so different from what we might bring today? Like all gifts, these speak both of the One to whom the gift is offered and of the one bringing the gift.

But Scripture also says that, before opening their treasures and offering them to the child, they "prostrated themselves and did him homage." Most of us have enjoyed both giving and receiving gifts over the years. Perhaps we have even taken time to remember why we give gifts. But have we also taken the time to give homage?

Jesus was born in a most unlikely place. The magi traveled a great distance, following a star in faith to find him. Are we ready to make a similar journey? In what unlikely darkness might we find the Child? And when we do will we also "do him homage?" Will we recognize him in the shopping mall? in the hospital emergency room? in a downtown office building?

Each of the wise men brought what he felt was most precious. What do we bring? The baby is waiting.

...With Compassion and Kindness

"Mommy track." "Daddy track." New language. A young woman attorney leaves a high-powered law firm where she is almost certain to make partner so that she and her husband can begin a family in Iowa. Men in a large corporation petition for a diaper change station in, of all places, the men's room! Daycare is again an issue in employment negotiations. Single parents demand increased flexibility in work hours so that they can be present to their children. That's one side of the story.

But then there's the other side. There's the new mother whose HMO allows only twelve hours in the hospital when she gives birth. There's the proposal that must be changed at the eleventh hour, even though Dad's promised to be at the Little League game. There's the middle-aged woman who, because her aging mother can no longer be left alone, must take time off from work to interview caregivers. There's the man whose father has developed Alzheimer's disease, necessitating a time-consuming search for a competent nursing home. What happens to their jobs while these things are going on?

"Those who honor their father atone for sins, and those who respect their mother are like those who lay up treasure" (Sir 3:3-4). Are these words only meant for the daughter or son involved? Couldn't they also apply to the employer or human resource person whose job it is to determine what benefits might be available? Couldn't they also apply to me when my help can make it possible for my colleague to take needed time for family leave? Aren't we all called to put on compassion and kindness?

In the Christmas season when we hear angelic messages of "peace on earth," and especially as we honor the Holy Family, perhaps each one of us might take a moment to ask what *we* are called to do as members of *God's* family...

...With Mystery

Midnight Blush

In the mystery of a moment
a Child is born.
A speck in time
and time will never be
the same again.

In a city hardly noted on the map,
to a couple far from home,
a night like any other night
becomes the dawn of time.

A new star rises in the east
like silent thunder breaking
through the velvet sky.
God's messengers proclaim
the Word made flesh.

Nestled in the hay a
baby cries; His mother smiles;
her husband stands in awe.
The weak and powerful
bow down together at the door.

The Holy Night is now.
A Child is born.
And in the mystery of a moment
we will never ever be
the same again.

CHAPTER 10

Taking a Time-Out

Rest—
Relax—
Have peace in your soul.

Drink long and cool
from the pool
of solitude.

Let fresh thoughts
enter your mind
and dance there—
Like flowers
dancing
on the hill.

Let sunlight play in your heart—
and the beauty and peace
of God's world
enter into
and become one
with you....

"And on the seventh day God finished the work that he had done, and he rested on the seventh day from all the work that he had done." (Gen 2:2). We are created in the image of a God who worked for six days, creating the heavens and the earth and all that is under the earth, and we are pretty good at working. But we are also created in the image of a God who rested on the seventh day from all the work he had undertaken and, unfortunately, most of us are not so good at resting.

Of all the addictions from which people suffer in our world, workaholism is the only one that is not only accepted but actually encouraged. When someone suffers from an addiction to drugs or alcohol we invite them to *join* a support group or *check into* a treatment center. When someone suffers from an addiction to work we invite them to *facilitate* a support group or *manage* a treatment center. And if you're looking for someone to work on your committee, ask a busy person to do it.

We are busy persons. And we'll work twenty-four hours a day, seven days a week, to prove it! Like the young attorneys in our office used to say, "Thank goodness it's Friday; only two more working days 'til Monday."

It's time for a time-out. Children nap. Cats snooze in the sun. Bears hibernate. Birds fly south. But the average worker? Like the Energizer bunny we just keep on going...and going...and going.

A friend of mine was taking a sabbatical. He wasn't happy about it. He wasn't good at relaxing. He had always felt the need to keep busy. He found his identity in his work. But now the university at which he was teaching had offered him a sabbatical—as a condition for future employment—and he was having a hard time with it. I wrote this poem as a kind of blessing prayer for him. Now I offer it to you.

...For Transformation

"The work of human hands...." Someone pointed out to me recently that these are the words the priest uses during the preparation of the gifts at Mass. These are the words we use to describe what it is we bring to our God, to be united with our God, to become God's own body and blood. We do not offer wheat and grapes, but bread and wine (Lk 22:17-20), "fruit of the earth and *work of human hands*."

None of us ever comes to the altar on Sunday empty-handed. We bring the other six days of our week with us. We bring our joys and our sorrows. We bring our laughter and our tears. We bring our moments of leisure—and we bring our work.

What is the work of your hands? Is it a legal brief? An annual report? Is it a balance sheet? Or a proof sheet? Is it a computer program? Or a dressing for a wound? Is it food prepared? Or shoes repaired? Is it a "widget" or a "whatchamacallit"?

What is the work you do to earn your daily bread? What is represented by the dollars you put into the collection basket to be taken up (along with the bread and wine) to the altar? What is it that you bring to lay on the altar, to become the Body and Blood of Christ? What is the work of your human hands?

...For Our Health

Paul is an attorney working for a large multinational law firm in the area of workers' rights. In that capacity he finds it necessary to travel several days out of each month. Recently Paul suffered a debilitating illness that required a prolonged stay in the hospital to be followed by three to four weeks of bed rest. However, since the firm was in the middle of a major case, the partner in charge indicated that it would be "helpful" if Paul could just attend one short, previously scheduled out of town meeting.

So Paul ignored his doctor's advice and left for Omaha. It was in the middle of the meeting that it happened. One minute he was standing in front of the group; the next he was lying on the floor surrounded by paramedics. Later, following emergency surgery, his doctor told him he was lucky to be alive.

"You shall love the Lord your God with all your heart, with all your soul, and with all your mind, and with all your strength" (Mt 22:37–39). Paul is a good man. He attends Mass every Sunday and occasionally on a weekday as well. He even chose his specific area of law in the belief that here he might serve God as well as humankind. Paul loves God. But there's more to the commandment.

"You shall love your neighbor...." The work Paul was doing was intended to protect the livelihood of several hundred people. If you had asked him about it he would have told you that the reason he drove himself the way he did was that he truly cared for those people.

"As yourself." But how might Paul have advised the people on whose behalf he was working, had they asked him how many hours they should work each week? Or how soon they should return to work following major surgery? The second part of the commandment assumes that we first love ourselves, body and spirit. God gifts us with the ability to love and care for ourselves. Only then can we love and care for one another.

How are we doing?

...For Renewal

"You shall love your neighbor as yourself" (Mt 22:39). Sometimes I wonder if we don't get so caught up in the "love your neighbor" part that we forget the "as yourself" part. Almost a year ago a friend of mine began working near my office as a massage therapist. As part of her initial marketing effort she sent me a coupon good for one free massage. I have yet to use it.

And I don't think I'm alone. One of the most difficult issues people deal with today is the issue of balance. The work week is getting longer. Add to that the amount of stress many people work under and you can see that there's not much "loving of self" going on. In fact, I suspect that most of us wouldn't treat our worst enemy the way we treat ourselves.

We get up while it's still pitch dark outside, fumble our way into the shower, dress hurriedly so as not to wake the rest of the household, then hop into the car, a piece of toast in one hand and a cup of coffee in the other, in a mad dash to the train station. After that there's a lengthy commute during which we sit with laptop running and cell phone at the ready. Once in town we maneuver our way through mobs of pedestrian traffic to get to the office, all of this before the sun has completely risen, only to repeat the pattern in reverse late in the evening long after the sun has set.

Most of us would never ask a neighbor to do this! In fact, we would probably counsel against it if someone came to us for advice in looking for a job. Managers provide wellness programs dealing with everything from diet to exercise to relaxation techniques while, in their own lives, the stresses of business are causing heart attacks and nervous exhaustion at an alarming rate. Far from being virtuous, in the end they find that their lack of "loving themselves" has indeed made them "aliens" in their own bodies.

Come to think of it, if you will excuse me, I have to go. You see, I have this coupon to redeem...

...For Relationship

It feels so good to be right. Perhaps that's why it can be so easy to fall into the trap of being righteous. Part of the problem is that what appears right to one may appear to another as being righteous. In Scripture the Pharisees are quite sure that they are right (Mk 2:18–22). And, based on Jewish law, they make a pretty good case. Jesus, on the other hand, has an entirely different understanding of what it means to be right.

Most of us have been raised to believe that it is right to work hard, and so we do—seven days a week. The only difference is that we go to church on Sunday. We keep Sabbath by doing what we think is the right thing. But Sabbath isn't about *doing*—it's about *being*.

Sabbath is about taking time to be in right relationship. We are to keep the Sabbath as a time of prayer so that we might be in right relationship with God. We are to forgive debts and be reconciled so that we might be in right relationship with one another. We are to let the land lie fallow so that we might be in right relationship with the earth.

We read the gospel events with the advantage of two thousand years of hindsight, and we wonder how the Pharisees could have been so blind. But what will people think two thousand years from now when they read about what *we* have—or have not—done? Will they remember us as people who celebrated Sabbath with joy? Or will they remember us as people who were so busy doing things right that we never really celebrated Sabbath at all?

...For Prayer

The contrasts between Job, Paul, and Mark are, for me, a study in *hope* (see Job 7:1–4, 6–7; 1Cor 9:16–19, 22–23; Mk 1:29–39). First we find Job, confused and angry. His affliction is seen by his friends as a punishment from God. His life has become drudgery, his days bereft of *hope*.

Later, in Mark's gospel, it initially seems that things haven't changed much. People continue to suffer. Simon's mother-in-law is described as being sick with fever, others as ill or possessed by demons. There is much human affliction. But look again. There is a new sense of hopefulness. The followers of Jesus gather the afflicted—the "whole town"—at his door for healing. Paul preaches affliction chosen, willingly, for the sake of others. In short, in light of Jesus' passion and resurrection affliction is no longer a reason for hopelessness. Rather, it has become an occasion for *hope*.

But how does this apply to us? Affliction is still with us. It hasn't gone away. For many, life still feels like drudgery. Poverty and disease still kill. Children still go to bed hungry. Truth be told, we usually feel more like Job than Paul. Where can we, in twenty-first century America, turn for *hope*?

Perhaps we can find some clue in Mark's gospel. Mark tells us that Jesus "went off to a deserted place" to pray. Jesus was human, like us in all things but sin. Like us, He knew what it meant to work long days, to be hungry and thirsty. Jesus knew human drudgery and affliction, sickness and pain. But Jesus also knew the necessity of prayer. In other words, Jesus knew where to turn for *hope*.

This same source of hope is available to us—if we choose it. In the midst of our busyness, when our life seems difficult and out of control, when our nights are troubled and our days beg for healing, Jesus invites us to come away with him to a quiet place to pray. But it's still our call. Hopeful? Or hopeless?

...For Family

In my home parish we take baptism seriously. And, with an average age of thirty-two, we have plenty of opportunities to demonstrate that. Believing as we do that it is through baptism that new members are brought into the Christian community, we do not schedule "private" baptisms. Rather, on the first full weekend of every month, at every Mass, we baptize and welcome new members into our community. Having been in the parish from its beginning I have often had the pleasure of getting to know the families who bring their children to be baptized. Robin's was one of those families.

I met Mike and Michelle (Robin's parents) shortly after our parish had been established. Of course Mike and Michelle didn't know each other yet, but that gets us ahead of our story. I was training lectors for our fledgling parish and Mike was in one of the first groups to go through the class. He was a quiet young man, just beginning to look seriously at this business of "spirituality." His interest in Scripture and liturgy led to many good conversations and a friendship developed between us as we got to know one another. A year or two later Michelle came into the program. And the rest, as they say, "is history." Theirs was one of the first weddings in our parish (most members were young married couples moving into the area). Now all they wanted was to have a baby to complete their family.

But as time passed, Michelle did not conceive. They began to think about adoption. And that's where Robin came into the picture. It took many months, and a few false starts, but last year this beautiful baby girl became the adopted daughter of Mike and Michelle. And since the entire faith community had been anxiously awaiting her arrival, it seemed only natural that the entire faith community should welcome her.

So it was that Robin was adopted into two families, beloved child of Mike and Michelle, beloved child of God, baptized "in the name of the Father, and of the Son, and of the Holy Spirit" (Mt 28:19). And all God's people said, "Amen!"

...For Gardening

Riding into the city on the train over the years I have watched a veritable forest of new apartment buildings and town homes spring up along the tracks. It's always especially exciting when they put in the landscaping. Suddenly the buildings begin to come alive with flowers and shrubs. But will the plants take root and grow in those narrow strips of earth, shaded by brick and concrete? Has the ground been properly prepared? Is it deep enough? Is there enough air and light? Or will the plants be choked by pollution and a lack of sunshine and rain?

Matthew's gospel describes something very close to those suburban gardens (Mt 13:1–23). In his gospel Matthew paints a vivid word picture. We can almost see the sower scattering the seed. Plants seem to spring up overnight, much like the trees and shrubs planted in the tiny gardens between the buildings. And there is the same question: "Will they grow?"

Our lives can be like that, too. We put in landscaping, but whether and how the plants will grow depend as much on our DayTimer as it does on our good intentions. Often we're so busy with work and home responsibilities that there's little time left over to water the soil of our soul. In fact, we can get so caught up in a tangle of activity that we're not even aware that our life of faith is being choked out. The noisiness of Monday through Saturday keeps us from hearing the seed of God's Word proclaimed on Sunday. And the question remains: "Will it grow?"

Our city planners believe that plants can grow and thrive in the middle of the city. We believe that God's Word can grow and thrive in the midst of the ordinariness of our lives. But like those city planners, we too must do our part. We must prepare the soil of our days. We must feed and water the seed of God's Word planted in the garden of our soul. Jesus assures us that if we do these things we will indeed bear fruit and yield many times over. In the words of the children's nursery rhyme, "How does your garden grow?"

...For Life

"Today that I have set before you life and death.... Choose life so that you and your descendants may live" (Deut 30:19). I am struck by the fragility of life. This week I am again made aware of how precious and uncertain life can be. The sister-in-law of a close friend suffers a major stroke and remains on life support in a drug-induced coma. Another friend, a husband and father, newly ordained a deacon, is diagnosed with an inoperable brain tumor. To treat or not to treat? Questions of length of days vs. quality of life. A well-known sports figure finds his life depends on the generosity and willingness of a total stranger to be an organ donor. The list goes on and on, far beyond the space available here. No doubt you have names and faces of people you care for in your mind as your read this. The gift of life—so precious and yet so fragile.

We thank God for the gift of life, but do we really *live* our lives? Rushing through my house this morning, preparing for work, I pass a window and my heart stops for one aching moment as I catch sight of the electric stain of sunrise spreading across the sky. Standing on the platform waiting for my train I close my eyes to more fully enjoy the wind washing my face with just an edge of spring in its touch.

Life, in all its wonder, surrounds us. We are immersed in it. In the warmth of spring, in the chill of autumn; when the morning sun rips open the fabric of the sky and at the end of day when the coverlet of darkness is drawn again and the earth surrenders to sleep. Life, "what God has prepared for those who love him" (1Cor 2:9).

...For Blessing

This morning as I walked to St. Peter's Church from the train station St. Francis of Assisi's "Canticle of the Creatures" came to mind. Well, actually, one verse of the Canticle came to mind (the only verse I've been able to memorize, despite numerous attempts to memorize it all).

The morning was windy and rainy, more early spring than early summer, and the words I remembered were, "Be praised, my Lord, for Brother Wind, and for the air, and for the clouds; for azure calm and all climes, by which You give life to Your creatures." At least that's the way I first memorized it. However, there are varying translations of the Canticle and the one I have come to prefer reads, "through whom You *cherish* Your creatures." I really like the word "cherish."

In the desert Southwest where I was born clouds are few and far between. The sky can seem almost relentlessly sunny and the sight of even one cloud on the horizon, with its hoped-for promise of rain, becomes a cause for celebration. That's kind of what I was feeling this morning.

Granted, at first glance the idea that the wind that nearly takes my breath away as I cross the Chicago River is an expression of God's cherishing me may not be readily apparent. But when I really think about it, especially in these days of concern over holes in the ozone layer and as we anticipate another summer with the air hanging brown and heavy over the city and humidity pinning our clothes to our bodies, then the thought of even the tiniest breeze becomes a welcome relief.

As I continue to ponder Francis' words I'm reminded of another *Wind*. In the reading from the Acts of the Apostles proclaimed on Pentecost Sunday, Luke talks about "a sound like the rush of a violent *wind*" (2:2). "Be praised, my Lord, for Brother *Wind*." Could it be that Francis is talking about something deeper? Could our experience of desert dryness have less to do with the weather than with that dryness of spirit experienced by the Samaritan woman (Jn 4:5–42)? Is it possible that the desert that cries out for water is not in the Southwest at all but, rather, inside us? Does this *Wind* that Francis calls upon to praise God carry, not rain, but the promise of living water to lift the heaviness and wash away the pollution that is within, rather than outside, each one of us?

When I left my house this morning I had to turn on my headlights to penetrate the fog. As my train approached the city the Sears Tower was shrouded in mist and it was as though the tops of the taller buildings had simply evaporated. As I write these words the same wind that whipped my coat around my legs this morning has blown the fog away and replaced it with heavy clouds. The buildings that seemed so insubstantial earlier now stand firm and solid. A steady rain is falling and the dry, cracked ground drinks it in. Potted flowers and trees turn green before our eyes. The wind has brought the earth back to life.

Perhaps Francis' words aren't really so different from Luke's after all! "Be praised, my Lord, for Brother *Wind*." Words of praise—and of blessing. When we are weak the power of this Wind will strengthen us. When we fall the force of this Wind will support us. In the storms of our lives this Wind will bring calm. This is the Spirit that rushed upon the disciples on that first Pentecost; this is the Wind that gave them life and the courage to go out and give praise to God…

Be praised, my Lord, for Brother Wind
through whom You cherish Your creatures.

...For Weeds Growing on the Roof

There are weeds
growing on the roof.

Planted by the wind—
watered by the rain—
called into being
by God's own hand.

Looking to no man
to tend them.

Sturdy harbingers of spring,
sentinels of summer.

Bountiful harvest for birds
in asphalt desert.

Food and shelter for insects
buffeted by city winds.

Grasping at life
through tarpaper cracks.

There are weeds…
growing…
on the roof…

...For Awareness

"Patchy fog," they call it. But I can't see my hand in front of my face! My car headlights don't even begin to penetrate. The fog is as thick as the proverbial pea soup. I'm forced to slow down to a crawl. Driving along the country roads, I pray that the other drivers will have their headlights on so that I can see them behind the white wall. Rush hour. Driving to the train. Cars coming off side roads, backing out of driveways. I watch my speed, eyes burning, straining to pierce the cloud.

This is the Gathering Rite, the "coming-together ritual." Headlights, brakelights, and turn signals—the ritual of hospitality. Riding to the train—the entry rite. Then—our work.

We have come to the workplace, reverencing the lives of others. We emerge from the fog. Can we bring that same care to this workday world? Can we signal our intentions beforehand, avoiding any sudden change of course? Can we continue to look out for the lives and safety of our fellow travelers on this road of life as we have on the back roads and by-ways of our towns? Can we reverence the person as we do have his automobile?

Where is the fog in our lives? And who are the other drivers?

...For Transfiguration

Before moving to Wisconsin my husband and I lived in a small suburb outside of Chicago. I used to drive twenty minutes to the train station before boarding a commuter train for the Loop in downtown Chicago. One morning, on my way to the train station, I had an incredible experience. I saw the sky transfigured before my eyes! The clouds seemed to be on fire, and in the middle of it all was one blinding shaft of light connecting earth with heaven. It was all I could do to keep my car on the road. I wanted to pull over, to hold on to the moment. But then the colors began to fade. Sunlight washed over the world. And I continued on my way.

Abram also had an incredible experience (Gen 15:5–12, 17–18). It was an experience of God. Like me, he would have liked to "pull over" and hold on to the moment. But God had something else in mind. God called him to leave the comfort and familiarity of the moment, to leave his father's house and to step out in faith. God promised to bless Abram, and Abram trusted God's promise. Abram continued on his way.

Each of us is called. We are called as parents and children, spouses and friends, neighbors and workers, teachers and students, healers and those seeking healing. When and if a "transfiguration moment" occurs we must listen to what it says, but we must not seek to "build tents" there. Like the disciples, we must come back down from the mountaintop and return to our communities (Lk 9:28B–36).

Our call is to work in the world so that it might be transformed. This is where our "holy life" is lived out. The sunrise is gift and blessing, but our call is not to stay there. Our call is to bring the blessing down from the mountaintop and to share its light with the world. God calls us to build up the kingdom, to step out in faith, to continue on our way.

...For Hunting and Fishing

In the upper-Midwest where I live there are really only two seasons—hunting season and fishing season. Work schedules and vacation plans, weddings and baptisms, even Mass schedules are planned around them. About now it's the season for fishing, usually conducted from small shanties set out on the ice on one of the dozens of small lakes in the region. Long winter nights lend themselves to sorting tackle and tying flies and there's nothing like meeting up with a bunch of fishing buddies to share stories over a cup of coffee and a plate of bacon and eggs at the corner café.

Fishing was also very important along the shores of the Sea of Galilee. Surely, then as now, long hours were spent telling stories while the men mended their nets and prepared to set out, the gentle rhythm of boats rocking in the water healing their fatigue. So it was to this place that Jesus came after hearing the news of his cousin John's arrest. And it was from this place that Jesus called those who would be his followers (Mt 4:12–23).

Where would Jesus go today? Probably, as he did two thousand years ago, He would go to where the people are. He would go into the woods in the fall and invite the hunters to hunt for new ways to build the kingdom. He would sit in the ice shanty and listen to the stories. He would rise at dawn, dress in the dark, and make his way down a gravel road to a community dock where men and women were uncovering and preparing their boats. He would sit with them for hours through the heat of the day batting flies and mosquitoes. And he would invite them to follow him.

Jesus continues to hunt for followers in duck blinds and ice shanties. He calls us where we are, at work and at play, in all the seasons of our lives, and invites us to become fishers of men and women. "The kingdom of heaven is at hand." The question is, how willing are we to leave our nets and follow him?

...For Unexpected Surprises

Expectations, or the lack of them, can become self-fulfilling prophecies. Elizabeth was well beyond childbearing age; it would have been natural for Zechariah to have given up any expectations of ever being a father (Lk 1:5–17). David was the youngest, and least likely, of Jesse's sons to be chosen as king (1 Sam 16:6–13). Mary was a virgin and, in the natural course of events, should not have become pregnant (Lk 1:26–38). But God had other expectations.

"The Lord called me from birth…." Isaiah the prophet and King David, John the Baptist and Mary of Nazareth, were all called from birth. God had certain expectations for them. We read their stories in the Scriptures and hear them proclaimed at Eucharist.

But what about their parents? What about *their* expectations? Zechariah may have expected John to follow in his footsteps in the Temple. Jesse probably expected David to tend the sheep. Mary's parents may have been looking forward to grandchildren, but certainly they could have had no idea what that would mean. God's expectations, it seems, are often very different from our own.

The parents of Dr. Rachel Naomi Remen, author of *Kitchen Table Wisdom*, were both doctors. They expected that she, too, would practice medicine. What they did not expect was that she would go on to become a spiritual writer. Dorothy Day set out to be a reporter. When she began marching in the cause of equality she certainly never expected to found the Catholic Worker Movement. As a young student, Jonas Salk could not have expected that one day his research would virtually eliminate polio. And Cesar Chavez probably did not expect to become a leader in the pursuit of justice for the migrant worker. Sometimes God's expectations surprise us.

Sometimes God calls us to put aside previous expectations—family expectations regarding a career path, cultural expectations of fame and fortune, or even the expectation that we are to have no expectations! The Lord has formed each one of us from the womb and calls each of us by name. God has great expectations for us. But then, what did we expect?

...For Gathering Gifts

Since Vatican II we have begun referring to those gathered for Eucharist as the "assembly." In the Scriptures we hear Nehemiah use the same word to describe a group of "both men and women and all who could hear with understanding" (Neh 8:2), a description which could as easily describe our own gathering for worship. We also call this gathered assembly of the baptized the Church, the people of God, and the Body of Christ, a phrase that might come directly from Paul's Letter to the Corinthians where he compares those baptized in one Spirit to parts of the one body of Christ (1 Cor 12:12–30).

But what are these "parts" that Paul talks about? Perhaps an example will help. Shortly after moving to Wisconsin my husband and I decided to build an addition to our house. First we met with the contractor. He, in turn, contacted an excavator and someone to pour the foundation. Next came carpenters, roofers, plumbing and heating experts, electricians, painters, tile and carpeting people, and so on. Each person was necessary. Each brought his or her own gifts and talents. Another example. Last week I visited my doctor and my dentist. Each comes highly recommended, but I wouldn't think of asking either of them to build my room addition. While they also bring gifts, theirs are different gifts.

Sometimes we are tempted to think of the Church only as the hierarchy, or as a building. We go to church. We look to the Church to tell us what to do, how to think. We forget that, while clergy and religious have specific gifts, they are no more necessary than our own. For instance, I would not want Father to fill my tooth (unless Father also happens to be a dentist) or to install my plumbing. But I would be very uncomfortable if I had to live with my toothache (or without indoor facilities!).

The next time you gather with the assembly to celebrate Eucharist look around at the many and unique gifts that are present and ask yourself, "What special gift do I bring to build up the Body of Christ? How am I Church?"

...For Rest

In 2000 we celebrated a year of Jubilee, and one aspect of a year of Jubilee is Sabbath. In Mark's gospel Jesus stresses the need for Sabbath (Mk 6:30–34). The apostles have just returned from having been sent out to preach and heal. As they begin to tell Jesus about all they have done He invites them to ""Come away to a deserted place...and rest a while."" Jesus knows that, if they are to be of service to the world to which they are sent, they must first take care of themselves.

In her book, *My Grandfather's Blessings*, Rachel Naomi Remen writes, "One of the fundamental principles of real service is taught many times a day aboard every airplane in the United States....It is the part just before takeoff when the [flight attendant] says, 'If the cabin loses pressure, oxygen masks will fall from above. Put your own mask on first before you try to help the person next to you.'" We cannot be of service to one another if we're on the verge of nervous collapse ourselves! The command in Scripture is to "love your neighbor as yourself," but most of us wouldn't treat our worst enemy the way we treat ourselves.

I know a lawyer who routinely works from sixty to eighty hours a week. In his mid-thirties he had a pacemaker implanted; in his mid-forties he faced cancer surgery. He was the first attorney in the firm to make a phone call from an airplane, and the story of how he once jumped onto a plane as it was pulling away from the jetway is legendary. But his wife, a very wise woman, recognizes his need for Sabbath. Once a year she plans a vacation someplace where there are no telephones or airplanes. In other words, she invites him to "come away...rest awhile."

Jesus invites us to do the same. It is an invitation to Sabbath.

CHAPTER 11

Peace Be With You...

"Peace I leave with you—
my peace I give to you."

But where is this peace?

On paper treaties—signed by paper kings?
In words—spoken by tongues choked with too many words?

Peace does not live on paper—
or in crooked words.

In dollars, then? Endless dollars
stolen from the poor—the lame—
the young—the ill—
the homeless?
Dollars printed with blood and sealed with the seal of clay gods?

Peace cannot be purchased with coins—
nor bartered for in closed rooms.

The peace that Jesus promised has already been purchased—
bought and paid for
with the blood of the Lamb.

A peace so simple—
yet impossible for some to see.

It is in love that we find peace.
Love of God above all things;
love of neighbor as myself.

"Thy kingdom come."
The kingdom here—but not yet.
The kingdom we must build.
The kingdom—of peace.

I t was the Feast of Pentecost, the event that, according to some Scripture scholars, was intended to reverse what had happened at Babel. At Babel human pride resulted in chaos and fighting. People no longer spoke the same language. They could neither understand one another nor could they make themselves understood.

On Pentecost divine intervention brought order and peace. "Now there were devout Jews from every nation under heaven living in Jerusalem. And…each one heard them speaking in the native language of each" (Acts 2:5–6). It would seem that a key requirement for peace is communication. Human beings have problems with communication. Perhaps that's why we have such problems with peacemaking.

In the Hebrew Scriptures we find that tensions have existed in the Middle East for thousands of years. But we don't need to look that far from home to realize that the problem of peace, or the lack thereof, isn't limited to any one part of the globe. In spite of all that modern technology has made possible, there is still little peace among us. Nations go to war because of differences in the way they are governed. Nations go to war because of differences in the way they structure themselves economically. Father wars against son; brother wars against brother; the rich war against the poor.

People even go to war because of differences in the way they worship. Christians war against Muslims; Muslims war against Jews; Catholics war against Protestants; liberals war against conservatives; fundamentalists war against evangelicals—the list goes on and on, all in the name of God. It seems there is no end to the reasons people give for going to war.

"Peace I leave with you; my peace I give to you. I do not give to you as the world gives" (Jn 14:27). The world gives peace, but then the world takes it away again. God does not give peace as the world gives peace. God's peace is everlasting. But where is this peace that God gives? I believe that it's right here. I believe that it's in the eyes of a child, the scent of spring, the rising of the sun, the song of a bird. I believe that the peace that God gives is incredibly simple—yet impossible for some to see. God's peace, God's kingdom, here—but not yet. The kingdom we must build; the kingdom of peace.

...In Our Nation

Scripture gives us two wonderful images for the Fourth of July. First, in the book of the prophet Zechariah we are told: "He will cut off the chariot from Ephraim and the war horse [machines of war] from Jerusalem...he shall command peace to the nations" (Zech 9:10). And in Matthew's gospel, we hear Jesus' invitation, "Come to me, all you that are weary and are carrying heavy burdens, and I will give you rest" (Mt 11:28).

Jesus calls those who "labor and are burdened" and offers rest. As workers in a nine-to-five (or nine-to-six or nine-to-seven) world we can certainly identify with this. Jesus could be talking directly to us! But then he goes on to say, "Take my yoke upon you." What could that possibly have to do with us? It might make sense in a farming community, but in Chicago? Other than a few leftover fiberglass cows scattered around the Loop there's nothing here to be "yoked" to, is there? And even if there is, we're not "yoked" to it, are we?

But think again. Our forebears declared their freedom from England and established an independent nation, protecting the rights of its citizens. On July Fourth we celebrate our Independence Day, and we remember the words on which our country was founded: "That all men are created equal, that they are endowed by their Creator with certain unalienable rights, that among these are life, liberty, and the pursuit of happiness."

In the Declaration of Independence our ancestors promised "liberty and justice for all." Maybe this is the connection. Jesus calls us to declare our freedom from sin and to establish the reign of God, protecting the rights of the "little ones," bringing liberty and justice to the marginalized and the oppressed. Have we become so "yoked" to some political party or economic system that we have forfeited our freedom to follow the Spirit?

In the gospel Jesus promises a "yoke that is easy" and a "burden that is light." "We hold these truths to be self-evident." Do we? Are they?

...In Our Families

Not long ago many of us found ourselves spending hours glued to our radios and television sets following the story of Elián Gonzalez, a little boy from Cuba, and of the way the United States government had finally decided to deal with the custody battle that surrounded him. We saw the photographs, over and over again, of an armed soldier entering the locked room where the child was hidden, demanding he be handed over, and of a woman carrying the little boy to a waiting vehicle. And we heard the stories.

But which story were we to believe? If seeing is believing, why is it often so difficult to know what to think? Opposing voices, some calm and reasoned, others raised and pleading to be heard. Which were we to listen to? Whose version of what happened were we to accept?

Thomas had a similar dilemma (Lk 24:35–48). Jesus was dead. It had been three days. But the women who had gone to the tomb had found it empty. And Peter had confirmed it. Now they were telling him that they had seen the Lord. Reason said that this was not possible. Who was he to listen to?

Different situations, but perhaps we can draw a comparison, or at least draw out some common elements. As I sit writing this column a calm seems to have descended on the Elián Gonzalez story. After being separated for months the little boy was reunited with his father, and he appeared to be enjoying at least some degree of peace. Peace—one of the gifts of the Holy Spirit; the first word Jesus spoke to the disciples. Having been reunited with his Father Jesus entered the locked room where the disciples were hidden and brought with him the gift of peace.

Our world is filled with opposing voices. How do we decide which to believe? Jesus' criteria seems clear. Does the decision bring life? Does it unite us with God and bring us peace? Or does it keep us hidden in our locked rooms of doubt and fear, demanding to see signs before we will believe?

...In Our Workplace

"Immorality, lust, hatred, rivalry, jealousy, selfishness, dissension, factions, envy, orgies." In his book, *Answers from Within*, Fr. Bill Byron suggests that, with the possible exception of orgies, this might pretty well describe the workplace as many of us experience it! But what would the workplace look like if, instead, we were to introduce love, joy, peace, patience, kindness, generosity, faithfulness, gentleness, and self-control?

The Pentecost readings point to two qualities that are essential if we are to live life to the full—communication and reconciliation. The believers speak in different languages, yet their hearers are able to understand them (Acts 2:1–11). There is shared communication and an absence of division.

"Peace be with you." Jesus says this, not once, but twice in the Pentecost reading from John's gospel (20:19–23). How are we to achieve this "peace"? By choosing to love and forgive those who have sinned against us; by loving, even when we don't "feel" like it; by being patient, or kind, or gentle, even in difficult situations. The love of Christ shows itself when we choose to practice self-control and drive on rather than giving in to "road rage" when someone cuts us off on the highway. We experience the peace of Christ when we choose to remain faithful to promises and committed to our word rather than renege when it might seem to our advantage to do so.

When we live in such a way that priority is given to material values over the values of the Spirit, we set ourselves up for separation and division, but when we choose to share the gifts of the Spirit with those around us we invite communication and connection. When we begin to understand and appreciate our differences, not as a threat to unity but rather as the rich gift of complementarity that God intends, we begin to experience the kind of peace that Jesus promises. The choice is ours. To build up the kingdom in peace and unity? Or to allow divisiveness and discontent to tear it apart?

...In Our Neighborhoods

It's called "racial profiling" and we are hearing a great deal about it on the news these days. Prior to September 11, 2001, term usually referred to what some saw as a tendency on the part of law enforcement officers to target certain classes of persons, often African and Hispanic Americans, for investigation without cause. More recently the term has been associated with the practice of routinely stopping and questioning people from the Middle East, especially in airports and at large public gatherings.

During World War II the term, had it been in use at that time, might have applied to Japanese-Americans. At other times in our history it might have applied to the Irish, the Chinese, Germans, Italians, and Eastern Europeans. In fact, even as our country celebrates unity in diversity, there is hardly a group of people who have not at some point in time been subjected to some form of racial profiling. It seems it is in our nature to fear the "other."

The Corinthians were no different. In Paul's First Letter to the Corinthians we hear the apostle reminding the community that "all those who in every place call on the name of our Lord Jesus Christ" are called to be holy (1:1–3). Evidently they, too, were suspicious of "others."

Today European currencies are merging. International business is conducted in a common language by individuals oceans apart via teleconferencing. Air travel is faster and more available than ever before in our history. Yet even as national borders dissolve in a shrinking world, billions of dollars are expended each year to defend those borders. It is almost as though, the more we come together, the more we feel we must distance ourselves from one another.

Perhaps, then, it is not so difficult after all to understand why we are so slow to accept that one "Lamb of God, who takes away the sin of the [whole] world." Could it be because we are also not willing to accept that we may be as much a part of that sinful world as is the "other"?

...In Our Social Gatherings

"Oops! Your baptism is showing."

It was one of those office parties where people who normally wouldn't exchange two words find themselves making small talk over a tray of cheese and crackers. Somewhere between the appetizer and dessert the conversation came slowly but inexorably around to the current war on terrorism. Sheri had been afraid that this moment might come..

The noise level was increasing. "Certainly we don't want to see innocent people die, but that's the price you pay when you go to war." Sheri began to fear that war might erupt right there in the conference room but, nervous as she was, she knew she had to speak. "He will not cry or lift up his voice, or make it heard in the street..." (Isa 42: 2).

Sheri expressed her concern that war might hurt, rather than help, the situation. She had read a good deal about what constituted a "just war" and wasn't at all sure that the current situation met the criteria. Forks stopped in midair. How dare she say such a thing! But Sheri went on. She told the other guests how she cried when she saw the youthful faces of soldiers sending holiday greetings home from overseas. "I have called...I have given you as a covenant to the people, a light to the nations,...to bring out from the prison those who sit in darkness" (Isa 42: 6–7).

"The enemy hates us. We can't just lay down and let them run over us," one of her co-workers insisted. But by now the trembling in her voice had all but disappeared and Sheri responded, "If we continue to meet hatred with hatred, where will it end? If not here—where? If not now—when?" "You know the message he sent to the people...preaching peace by Jesus Christ" (Acts 10:34).

Sheri was afraid. She knew that she didn't have all the answers, but as a baptized Christian she knew she must not let her fear control her. Sheri believed that God was more powerful than her fear. After all, wasn't that what Christmas was all about? Baptized into Christ's death and resurrection, hadn't she also been baptized into His life? "And a voice came from the heavens, saying, "And a voice from heaven said, 'This is my [daughter], the Beloved, with whom I am well pleased" (Mt 3:17). Is anybody listening?

…In Our Towns and Villages

In the painful days of mourning immediately after September 11, 2001, the citizens of our great nation came together in prayer as never before. TV cameras captured images of prayer services around the world: young people on college campuses, statesmen in historic cathedrals. As a nation we wept and prayed together. We remembered those who had lost their lives. And we prayed for peace.

But there were also other images. In my little town there was the presence of police cars in gas stations as long lines of cars hurried to fill up. It was rumored that gasoline prices would go to $2, $3, or even $4 per gallon, and in some cases they did. ""When will the new moon be over so that we may sell grain…?" (Amos 8:5). There was the image of a Molotov cocktail tossed through the windows of a mosque. "And the Sabbath, that we may display the wheat?"

We saw images of heroic men and women, good stewards who continued to do what was necessary without counting the cost despite the fact that, in so doing, many paid the ultimate price. We prayed for the courage to make wise decisions, knowing that our actions would affect the lives of people around the world, that we might fix our scales for justice and not for cheating. As we set a new course for our nation we prayed that we would not focus our energies on filling up our gas tanks and hoarding our wheat while sending the poor away barefoot. Like Paul, we directed our "supplications, prayers, intercessions, and thanksgivings…for kings and all who are in high positions" (1 Tim 2:1–2). We prayed that in these trying times we might be found trustworthy.

We saw so many images—the ghastly bloom of flames in the sky, tear-streaked faces holding photos of smiling loved ones, piles of rubble that were once towers of commerce, and people of faith gathered in prayer. Broken and bleeding we came together, lifting up holy hands "without anger or argument" in churches, synagogues and mosques—and together we prayed for peace.

...In Our Financial Institutions

I know that I am not alone in observing that since September 11, 2001, everything has changed. Nothing is the same. I am reminded of the Scripture story of the rich man and Lazarus (Lk 16:19–31). In this story the rich man (we are not told his name—perhaps he is so rich that everyone knows him) lives his life unaware of the poverty of Lazarus at his door. Prior to September 11, when we read this story we might have drawn a parallel to some third world country. But it is not prior to September 11, and nothing is the same.

Those events, horrific as they were, can teach us—if we will only learn from them. During the days and weeks immediately after the attack there was an outpouring of care for survivors in New York City and Washington, DC. An e-mail I received noted that, covered with dust and grime, we are all one color; and with the blood of donors flowing in victims' veins, we are all one body. In ways no one could have predicted or chosen the chasm between rich and poor was eliminated. We had become one people.

But what about tomorrow, and all the tomorrows after that? CNN coverage continues to open our eyes to conditions, not only in New York City and Washington, DC., but also in Afghanistan and the Middle East. Even if it were possible for the victims of the tragic attacks to come back from the dead they could hardly speak more eloquently of the need to develop a global consciousness. As Wall Street continues to struggle for recovery have we changed our views regarding who profits from, and who is penalized by, trade policies? As small business owners are forced to decide whether to rebuild or go under, do we reconsider tax laws that benefit some more than others? We have redefined the word "hero." Will the change be reflected in salaries and benefits for public servants?

We have paid an incredible price. Let us pray to God that our hearts have grown. The victims have spoken with their lives—and we must never be the same.

...In Our Trade Negotiations

A message came across my desk recently regarding an e-mail forum on the crisis of third world debt. The forum was scheduled to coincide with summit meetings in Genoa, Italy, involving the heads of the world's eight leading industrial nations ("G-8"). The third world debt crisis, described as "one of the most disturbing issues within the debate over globalization," involves hundreds of billions of dollars lent to poor countries since World War II. While much of this money was lent in the name of democracy, freedom, and development, their inability to repay this debt has left some forty-seven countries, all but ten of them African, caught in a web of debt and poverty.

The $422 billion owed breaks down to approximately $380 per person, an impossible figure for governments of debtor nations, already mired in poverty, to repay. Creditor governments have offered to cancel up to fifty-five percent of the debt with the understanding that market-oriented "structural adjustment" economic policies and poverty-fighting plans be put into place. Besides, since much of the debt set for cancellation would never have been repaid anyway, some feel that forgiveness of the debt won't make much of a difference either way. On the other hand, there is also the legitimate concern that such policies may simply serve to get corrupt dictators off the hook.

Each side has expectations, some of them unrealistic. Yet each persists in asking. Debtor nations ask for a fish. Citizens of some of the poorest countries in the world ask for an egg. Do we give them a scorpion? "Give us each day our daily bread." Jesus taught us to say these words, but these words do not belong to us (Lk 11:1–13). People in debt-ridden nations, people whose children are dying from malnutrition and inadequate health care, also pray these words. "Whatsoever you do to the least of my brothers and sisters...." These are difficult questions. There are no easy answers. But we must at least get up and open the door.

...In Our World

For the Jews of Jesus' time tradition held that there were seventy-two nations in the world. In sending out the seventy-two on mission Jesus was, as it were, extending the good news of peace to the entire world (Lk 10:1–12, 17–20). Thus, with this in mind, you might say that Luke's gospel is really about "globalization."

Today, however, globalization looks a little different. Today, instead of simplicity and detachment we extend market expansion and increased consumer demand. Today, instead of peace we extend increased military spending. Today, in spite of the fact that justice says "the laborer deserves his payment," globalization opens the way for corporations to move to countries where labor is cheap and the dignity of the worker is a non-issue. Today, it is more often increased profits than increased healthcare that determines whether a business remains in the region or shakes the dust from its feet and relocates to a cheaper labor market.

What determines the shape of globalization? Perhaps we need to ask, "In whose name do we act?" That earlier globalization was done in the name of Jesus. Too often today's globalization is done in the names of the corporations that remain as companies merge and small business owners, unable to compete, simply disappear. Even the family farm is becoming a thing of the past. Today globalization is done in the names of countries that achieve independence and, almost as quickly, lose it as new wars spring up over land use and mineral rights with little concern for historical land ownership or environmental issues, and as ancient conflicts continue, funded to no small extent by unnamed powers that stand to gain financially from their lack of peace.

When they returned from those early efforts at globalization the seventy-two reported all that was done in Jesus' name. Today there are other names. But this doesn't have to be the way the story ends. The seventy-two were sent out "like lambs among wolves," but when they returned it was with much rejoicing. In this current age of globalization we have the tools and capabilities to do even greater things—if only we will remember in whose name we do them...

CHAPTER 12

...And Also With You

Whirling...swirling...
plunging...soaring...
buffeted by winds on all sides.

Assailed by sound—
voices—
sirens—
chattering—
grinding—
emptying themselves on our ears.

Turning...twisting,
reaching...
grasping to hold our space.

Solid ground crumbles—
slipping...sliding...

We tumble through glistening stars.

Shining...fading...
falsely leading.
Smiling...laughing...jeering.

No stop...no end...
a rush of light and sound.

Too much to measure—
too heavy to hold.

Where do we go from here, when we leave our place of encounter with God—as Peter, James and John did following the transfiguration (Lk 9:28B–36). What do we do? When we come down from the mountaintop, whom can we tell? Who will understand our journey of the spirit?

These are some of the questions that this final poem asks. When we gather to celebrate Eucharist, when we are caught up in the Divine, it can feel like we are "whirling … swirling." But on Monday morning it's more like "plunging" than "soaring," and the wind speed picks up as the week goes on. Phones ring, fax machines spew papers on the floor, copiers jam, people appear at our door out of nowhere demanding our time. "Voices," "sirens," all manner of noises are continually "emptying themselves on our ears." In the midst of this "rush of light and sound," how can we possibly hear that still, small voice we've been told we should be listening for? It can all seem "too much to measure…too heavy to hold."

"Peace be with you…" (Jn 20:19–21); and also with you. It is the beginning of the sending. It is the end of the beginning. We have been washed in living water. We have been given bread from heaven. But now it is time to go back to our homes and our schools, our offices and our shops, our factories and our foundries. Now it's time to take what we have been given here, at the Source, out into the world so that next week we can again come to the Summit, bringing with all of us the work of our human hands.

Where are we to go? What are we to do? We have come with our hungers; now we go to feed the hungry. We have come, broken and bruised; now we go to heal the hurting. We have come, lost and afraid; now we go to comfort the afflicted. This is no time to stop. And this is certainly not the end.

"Peace be with you…" and also with you. Now we go in peace, to love and serve the Lord.

…In Thirsts Quenched

"Thirst"—the Scriptures talk a great deal about thirst. On the Sunday of the First Scrutiny those involved in the Rite of Christian Initiation of

Adults (RCIA) experience a Sunday of testing. It is a Sunday of asking, "For what do you thirst? From which well do you draw?"

In our society we tend to be more comfortable with the language of hunger than of thirst (perhaps because of our penchant for diets?). It's true that Lent, with its call to fasting, offers a good opportunity for experiencing hunger. But when, in this part of the country known for its many lakes and rivers, do we thirst?

One thought that comes to mind has to do with an expression we use quite often when we talk about our "thirst for knowledge." Especially in this information age, the "thirst for knowledge" drives more and more of us. In order to keep current we read everything from the *New York Times* to the *Wall Street Journal*. In fact, judging from the number of books and periodicals dedicated to new management styles, market trends, and technology, we are a very thirsty society indeed.

We run from one seminar to the next. We spend hours staying abreast of the latest trends. We continue to "test" the system and to "quarrel" with the results. And still we thirst. What's really going on here?

"Everyone who drinks of *this* water will be thirsty again, but those who drink of the water that I will give them will *never* be thirsty" (Jn 4:13–14). These words sound eerily familiar. Like the Israelites, we grumble and demand that society quench our thirst. Could this be the answer? Could it be that in trying to quench our thirst we, like the Samaritan Woman before us, find ourselves out in the heat of the day drawing water from the wrong well?

...In Services Rendered

These days we often hear about the "servant-leader." This expression is usually used to describe that manager who is willing to work alongside his or her employees and to listen to their issues and concerns. The idea sounds good. Unfortunately, however, it often turns out to be just one more way to try to get employees to produce more and complain less.

But there is another way to understand the servant-leader. We read about it in Matthew's gospel for Palm Sunday, the beginning of Holy Week. We enter Holy Week—the most sacred week of the Christian year—

walking beside a donkey, waving palm branches and shouting "Hosanna" (Mt 21:5–9). If we really want to learn what it means to be a servant-leader we might want to pay attention to the man riding on the donkey.

Isaiah's words introduce him (Isa 50:4–7). He is the servant-leader who will speak on behalf of the weary, who will hear the cries of the poor and oppressed. (Are the people in my office weary? Does my industry engage in oppression?)

Paul tells us that Jesus chose not to distance himself from the human condition. Rather, He entered into the experience, emptying himself of what it meant to be God in order to be filled with what it meant to be human (Phil 2:6–11). (What is the relationship between management and labor in my shop? Does the word "professional" more correctly describe me than the word "human"?)

On Palm Sunday we enter the church singing, the words "Behold, your king comes to you" in our ears; we leave the church in silence, the words "This is Jesus, king of the Jews" before our eyes (Mt 27:37). During Holy Week we will wash feet. We will tell our stories. We will light candles. We will baptize and confirm. We will have journeyed through another Lent. We will have prayed to be good servant leaders. The question, however, is this—when we return to work on Easter Monday morning, will anybody be able to tell the difference?

...In Changed Hearts

Many people, having completed the RCIA and having been baptized at the Easter Vigil, experience a special sense of being in the presence of God. They may even express a desire to enter a religious order or to take a job working for the church. Usually it is suggested that they wait a year or two before making such a choice. Then, if they still wish to pursue a religious vocation, they can inquire further. Most eventually realize that they are not called to religious life at all, that it's not their life that must change but their heart.

Peter, John, and James had a similar experience (Lk 9:28B–36). They had completed their ascent of the mountain with Jesus to pray when it happened. Jesus was transformed before their very eyes. They found them-selves standing in the presence of God. In their fervor they wanted to remain there, to build tents where they might spend their days in prayer. But, as with the newly baptized, this was not what God had in mind. Instead of remaining in isolation on the mountaintop they were to return to their community and there to continue to follow Jesus.

Mountaintops are wonderful places. And we might even find God there. But most of us are not meant to stay there. Rather, we are meant to contin-ue to follow Jesus back down the mountain and into all the ordinariness of our days. We are not meant to remain in the fervor of the moment but to be strengthened by it, not so much to be transformed as to transform.

Jesus knew he had further to go on his journey and that it would even-tually take him to the cross. Each of us must, in our own way, take that walk with him. The difference isn't in "where" we choose to live our lives but in "how." Can we stand with Jesus in the shadow of the cross? Can we find God in the faces of those who stand there with us?

...In Lives Unbound

On the Fifth Sunday of Lent those people who are preparing to come into the Church through the RCIA take part in the third of three rituals, or Scrutinies, as they are called. This particular Scrutiny includes an exorcism. The priest prays, "Free these elect from the death-dealing power of the spir-it of evil" or perhaps, "Rescue these elect from the tyranny of death," thus calling upon God to release those coming into the Church from death's power over them.

In John's gospel, Jesus prays for Lazarus' release from death (11:1–45). In his prayer that Lazarus might be released from death's power, however, Jesus does not act alone. Jesus says, "Lazarus, come out!," but only after telling the crowd to "take away the stone." Then, again, after Lazarus has been raised from the dead, Jesus instructs the crowd saying, "Unbind him, and let him go."

When we hear this reading we usually identify with Lazarus, and this is good since we, too, are bound by sin and dead to the Spirit. But what about those whom we bind up? What about those whose ideas we dismiss? What about those who so threaten us with their youth or intelligence or "whatever" that we feel compelled to roll the stone of dismissal across the opening of their door to opportunity, killing their spirit? How are they to be brought back to life?

Perhaps today Jesus is calling on us to "take away the stone" of jealousy, or rejection, or hypocrisy, and to "unbind" those whom we have bound by our actions and attitudes. Or perhaps it's our own life and goodness that we hold bound and in darkness simply because we fear the cost of being truly alive.

Take a moment to reflect on the prayers of exorcism. Where are we bound? How do we bind others? What stone must be rolled away so that, when Easter arrives, we may all share in the triumph of the Resurrection?

...In Restored Relationships

On the Fourth Sunday of Lent in Year B of the liturgical calendar we have the option of choosing our gospel from either John 3:14–21 (the traditional gospel for Year B) or John 9:1–41 (used in Year A or when the second scrutiny of the catechumens occurs). Both readings talk about light and darkness.

John 3:16 is by far the more familiar. "God so loved the world that he gave his only Son." In a world that preaches "you get what you pay for" this kind of news is almost unbelievable. God calls us to walk in the light—at no cost to us! But still it seems that some people prefer darkness.

In John 9:1–41 we hear the story of the man born blind and Jesus' use of the things of the earth to restore his sight. Dirt and saliva, the ingredients of healing, stuff that most of us consider worthless. "You get what you pay for" doesn't seem to work in this gospel, either.

A serpent raised on a pole pays the price so that the people who were bitten might be cured. A savior raised on a cross pays the price so that the people might regain their right relationship with God and with one another. We may not know a lot about snake bites in downtown Chicago but we certainly do know a lot about broken relationships. And we know that the kind of behavior that causes, or benefits from, broken relationships is often carried out in the darkness of the human heart. We know the temptation to turn a blind eye to business deals that ignore or dehumanize the human spirit. We know that sometimes it's better not to look too closely at what goes on around us for fear that it will bite us!

God wills life for *all* God's people, and life can only thrive in the light. On Ash Wednesday we heard the priest say, "Repent and believe." Do we believe? Do we really believe the incredible Good News of John 3:16? Because, if we do, it isn't enough for us to just hold up a sign at a Sunday afternoon baseball game. If we believe, we must be willing to ask ourselves this question: Is the work we do on Monday morning carried out in light? or in darkness?

...In New Ways of Seeing

I am a dinosaur. I admit it. In an age of e-mail I prefer "snail mail." Commuting on the train, surrounded by people working on laptops and talking on cell phones, I read my book or write in my journal. I pride myself on successfully transmitting a fax across town while the young adults I work with transmit information around the world via the internet. I am stuck being a dinosaur—and proud of it!

I suspect we all have areas of our lives where we are "stuck." Unfortunately, they're not all as neutral as being non-high tech in a computer age. That's why Jesus took on human form. He came to help us get "un-stuck"!

The prophet Isaiah's words echo, "Morning by morning he...wakens my ear to listen" (Isa 50:4)—but we don't hear. "Taking the form of a slave" (Phil 2:7) we hear—but we don't serve. "He humbled himself, became obedient" (Phil 2:8) we hear—but we are proud and demand our own way. We are invited to freedom—but we persist in being "stuck."

When we return to work on Easter Monday morning has our lenten journey into springtime have made any difference? Or do we too often find ourselves, like dinosaurs, stubbornly clinging to what binds us, still stuck in the darkness of winter?

…In Stones Thrown Down

Jesus has a way of showing up in the most unlikely places, especially in those places where we find ourselves locked in by fear.

Recently a group of us were discussing faith and the workplace. One young woman related that in her office they come together for Bible study at lunchtime. When I asked what they were studying, she responded that they had been reading the story of the woman caught in adultery (Jn 8:3–11). When I asked her what happened after they finished their lunch and went back to work she asked me what I meant. "I mean," I responded, "who do you throw stones at when you get back to the office?"

Recently I heard on public radio that in addition to the gay and woman bashing we've heard so much about lately there's a new wave of hate music making the rounds, this time targeted at African-Americans. And it isn't just rock and rap. In the short clip I heard on the radio a country singer drawled words I'd hoped we would never hear again. Yet there they were—malicious, hateful words—rocks intended to kill the spirit. Had this singer ever heard about stones? and tombs?

Recently we've begun to hear the word "militia" connected to "religious freedom." Unfortunately, some people even feel a need to throw stones at people who worship differently than they do. And it doesn't take long to go from throwing rocks to shooting bullets. Fear and self-righteousness can be dangerous drugs. Not only do they numb our brains but our hearts as well.

Each of us has our sack of rocks. We use them every time we make ourselves look good by making someone else look bad. We use them every time we hear someone complimented and respond with some negative gossip we've heard about him or her. We use them to stone reputations and opportunities. We use them to build walls of fear and separation, and then we fling more stones over the walls we have built.

We have the power to make peace or to make war, to throw rocks at one another or to drop them into the depths of God's forgiveness. The stone has been rolled away from the tomb. But there are other stones—and other tombs…

…In Hunger Satisfied

A friend of mine decided to make a major career change. A reduction of financial responsibilities in midlife allowed him the opportunity to change direction, even though it would mean starting over in a new field with a smaller salary. When he gave his notice his manager was surprised and suggested that they sleep on it and talk again in the morning.

The next day his manager called him into her office and, in an attempt to convince him to stay with the company, offered him an attractive raise, some stock options, a promotion that would allow for considerably more visibility in the corporation, and the very real possibility of moving into a corner office. My friend, while pleased and flattered, politely refused. He explained that he had to follow his passion, to do what he felt called to do. He assured his manager that it wasn't about money or power or prestige, but he could tell that she didn't really understand.

Jesus followed the Spirit into the desert to learn what he was being called to do (Mt 4:1–11). The devil came to tempt him with bread, power and prestige. Jesus refused. "Not by bread alone, but by every word that comes from the mouth of God does one live." The devil couldn't understand. He had spoken in the only language he knew, the language of the world. But Jesus spoke a different language. Jesus heard a different call.

Scripture tells us that Jesus was fasting and that he "was hungry." Lent is about fasting. Lent is about being hungry. Lent is about going out into the desert to face our hungers. When the tempter comes to us, what will he offer? What language will he speak? For what do *we* hunger?

…In Faith Restored

You might say that Thomas was a "bottom line" kind of guy. "Just the facts" could describe his approach to life. He would have fit right in at most corporate board meetings.

Or would he? A good businessperson, having established a basis in fact, moves to action. Jesus invited Thomas to put his finger in the marks in his hands, his hand in Jesus' side, but Scripture doesn't tell us how Thomas responded to that part of the invitation (Jn 20:19–31). We don't know if Thomas did, in fact, confirm the physical validity of the "facts."

What we do know is how Thomas responded to the second part of Jesus' invitation. After inviting Thomas to test his wounds Jesus went on to say, "and do not be unbelieving, but believe." Just imagine telling your investors that they should "not be unbelieving" when they request a prospectus. To comply with such a request would be out of the question. But Thomas did just that. Jesus offered him the opportunity to test the validity of the evidence. Thomas' response? "My Lord and my God!"

When we celebrate the Eucharist we believe that bread and wine become Jesus' body and blood. We respond with Thomas' words, "My Lord and my God." What we see does not change; bread and wine retain all the physical properties of bread and wine. Yet we believe in what we have not seen.

Lent is a time for unlocking doors; Easter is about Jesus entering, even though the door is still locked. Lent is about asking for proof; Easter is about believing based on the proof of an empty tomb. We are an Easter people. "Blessed are those who have not seen and have believed."

…In Mountaintops Revisited

"I have been to the mountaintop…." Dr. Martin Luther King, Jr., knew about mountaintops. But he didn't stay there. He knew about going up; and he knew about coming down. Abraham also knew about mountaintops. "Take your son…and offer him there as a burnt offering on one of the mountains that I shall show you" (Gen 22:2). Like Martin, Abraham knew about going up, and about coming down.

The mountaintop is where we traditionally think about finding God. If we conceive of heaven as being somehow "up," then it is logical to think that the higher up we go the closer we get to God. Unfortunately, this line of thinking has made us susceptible to the belief that our day-to-day life here on earth is farther away from God. So we, like Peter and James and John, look for ways to remain on the mountaintop (Mk 9:2–10).

It was on the mountaintop that Moses and Elijah met God. Jesus often went up to the mountaintop to pray. Jesus knew about going up—to Jerusalem, to Calvary. And Jesus knew about coming down, his body placed in the waiting arms of his mother. But Jesus knew something more. Jesus knew about resurrection.

What would have happened if Peter, James, and John had built their tents and remained on the mountaintop? I probably wouldn't be sitting here writing about their experience. Nor would you be reading my words. What if Martin had chosen to stay on the mountaintop? What would our world look like today?

Spiritual seekers have always sought the mountaintop encounter with God. But the true mystic knows that we are not meant to stay there. If the life, death and resurrection of Jesus Christ are to have any meaning in our world today it is up to us to bring its message back down from the mountaintop and into our homes and our communities, back to the places where we work and play. Are we builders of the kingdom? Or are we satisfied with being builders of tents?

...In Bread Broken

"Have you anything here to eat?" (Lk 24:35-48). This is hardly what we expect to hear Jesus saying so soon after the most incredible event in human history! It sounds more like what we would expect from our teenage children. Yet there it is. In order to prove that he is human, Jesus asks for something to eat. And the disciples come to believe.

This story comes right at the end of the Emmaus story. The two disciples who encountered Jesus on the road have just returned to Jerusalem to tell the others what has transpired when He appears in their midst saying, "Peace be with you." This greeting is too much for them. This greeting speaks of a divine reality that they simply can't understand. Yet Jesus puts it first—before food and the needs of the body, Jesus places peace and the needs of the soul. But the disciples can't relate to the first greeting. So Jesus asks for something to eat.

It was in the breaking of the bread that the two disciples on their way to

Emmaus came to know Jesus. It was when He offered them something to eat that they were able to identify the burning within them and finally, after the troubling events of the previous three days, find peace.

Now Jesus speaks to us. Do we respond with faith? Or, like the disciples, do we respond with disbelief? Do we understand that we too must go back to our lives—changed yet still the same—because that is precisely where we are to live out the Good News that Jesus has shared with us? Can we accept the responsibility that comes with the gift of the Resurrection? Do we understand what Jesus calls us to do? How do we respond to the stranger on the road when he asks, "Have you anything here to eat?"

...In Shadows Lifted

There is an assumption among some spiritual writers that if one believes in Jesus and lives a good life then fame and fortune will surely follow. Not only is this assumption dangerous, since it seems to say that the poor and powerless are somehow at fault for their situation, but, while people will sometimes try to use Scripture as their basis for believing this way, it simply is not borne out there.

In Mark's gospel Peter, James, and John are permitted a glimpse into eternity (Mk 9:2–10). Moses and Elijah, representatives of the prophets and the law, converse with Jesus. These two are among the most famous men in Jewish history, and to be in their presence was such a powerful experience that Peter immediately suggested it be commemorated with the building of three tents. Peter, understanding the experience only on a human level, wanted to make it permanent. He knew this was a mountaintop experience and he wanted to remain there.

But Jesus called him to a different mountaintop, Mount Calvary. Mark speaks not only of cloud but also of shadow. Spirituality, if it is truly grounded in Jesus Christ, must recognize both. Yes, Jesus may call us to the mountaintop. There may be times when things in our lives are going well. There may be experiences of such impact that we will want to capture them and give them permanence. But these experiences are not meant to be permanent. We must come down from the mountain. Followers of Jesus follow him, not just up to the mountaintop, but down into the valley of death.

The Good News is that even in that dark valley—when we find ourselves without power, when the job is eliminated, when loved ones die or move away, when our reputation is attacked, when we find ourselves most powerless—it is precisely then that Jesus reminds us that we will also experience his resurrection.

We are an Easter people. Alleluia is our song. And the Good News is that it has absolutely nothing to do with being rich or famous.

...In the Rest of Our Lives

I recently received an e-mail about skydiving. It seems that, just before his first jump, the student asked his instructor this question: "If, after I jump, my main chute fails to open, and if my back-up chute also fails to open, how much time do I have before I hit the ground?" The answer? "You have the rest of your life."

There is a passage from Luke's gospel that may not be as funny, but the message is similar (Luke 13:1–9). Life is messy. Unexpected things happen. While some of them may very well be the logical consequences of our actions (for example, one might ask if the skydiving student took all the necessary precautions in preparing his parachutes), others are totally impossible to predict. A child is born with a physical disability. A parent develops Alzheimer's. A family loses its home in a fire. Were they sinners? Probably so. Were they bigger sinners than we are? Probably not. But don't we still find ourselves secretly (or perhaps not so secretly) wondering what they did to deserve it?

Take it a step further. When I am the victim of misfortune don't I sometimes wonder what I did, or didn't do, to make God angry?

Moses ran away when he was accused of killing an Egyptian, surely a great sin (Ex 3:1–8A, 13–15). But Moses repented. And God chose him to lead the Israelites out of slavery. Our God doesn't inflict pain as punishment for sin. Our God calls us to repentance so that we might have life. Lent is about repentance, a special time set aside to "prepare our parachutes." This Lent will last forty days, just as it does every year, but not one of us can know for sure whether we will live to see Easter. Perhaps a tower will fall on us. Perhaps our parachute will fail. Will we be ready? How much time do we have to turn away from sin and believe the Good News? The answer is the same one the instructor gave his student. "We have the rest of our lives."

...In the Rising

The earth trembles and moves.
Light cracks the darkness.
A sound like rushing wind
tears around the edges of time.

Light centers to a single flame
rising out of death's deep pool.
Living water bubbles up
to overflow the rim of earth.

The wind takes on the wail of birthing
and labors forth into eternity
a new creation.

God's newly born—
our resurrection hope fulfilled—
we rise up laughing
in the
Alleluia Dawn!